CULTURESHOCK!

A Survival Guide to Customs and Etiquette

ARGENTINA

Fiona Adams

Marshall Cavendish
Editions

This edition published in 2007, reprinted 2008, by:
Marshall Cavendish Corporation
99 White Plains Road
Tarrytown, NY 10591-9001
www.marshallcavendish.us

Other Marshall Cavendish Offices:
Marshall Cavendish International (Asia) Private Limited. 1 New Industrial Road,
Singapore 536196 ■ Marshall Cavendish Ltd. 5th Floor, 32–38 Saffron Hill, London
EC1N 8FH, UK ■ Marshall Cavendish International (Thailand) Co Ltd. 253 Asoke,
12th Flr, Sukhumvit 21 Road, Klongtoey Nua, Wattana, Bangkok 10110, Thailand
■ Marshall Cavendish (Malaysia) Sdn Bhd, Times Subang, Lot 46, Subang Hi-Tech
Industrial Park, Batu Tiga, 40000 Shah Alam, Selangor Darul Ehsan, Malaysia

Marshall Cavendish is a trademark of Times Publishing Limited

ISBN 10: 0-7614-5397-0
ISBN 13: 978-0-7614-5397-0

Please contact the publisher for the Library of Congress catalogue number

Printed in China by Everbest Printing Co Ltd

Photo Credits:
All photos by the author except pages 18 (AFP); 3, 4, 9, 12–13, 20, 34, 40,
44, 48, 67, 72, 87, 92–93, 105, 117, 134, 137, 149, 162 (Photolibrary);
page 54–55 (Getty Images).
■ Cover photo: HBL Photo Network

All illustrations by TRIGG

ABOUT THE SERIES

Culture shock is a state of disorientation that can come over anyone who has been thrust into unknown surroundings, away from one's comfort zone. *CultureShock!* is a series of trusted and reputed guides which has, for decades, been helping expatriates and long-term visitors to cushion the impact of culture shock whenever they move to a new country.

Written by people who have lived in the country and experienced culture shock themselves, the authors share all the information necessary for anyone to cope with these feelings of disorientation more effectively. The guides are written in a style that is easy to read and covers a range of topics that will arm readers with enough advice, hints and tips to make their lives as normal as possible again.

Each book is structured in the same manner. It begins with the first impressions that visitors will have of that city or country. To understand a culture, one must first understand the people—where they came from, who they are, the values and traditions they live by, as well as their customs and etiquette. This is covered in the first half of the book.

Then on with the practical aspects—how to settle in with the greatest of ease. Authors walk readers through topics such as how to find accommodation, get the utilities and telecommunications up and running, enrol the children in school and keep in the pink of health. But that's not all. Once the essentials are out of the way, venture out and try the food, enjoy more of the culture and travel to other areas. Then be immersed in the language of the country before discovering more about the business side of things.

To round off, snippets of basic information are offered before readers are 'tested' on customs and etiquette of the country. Useful words and phrases, a comprehensive resource guide and list of books for further research are also included for easy reference.

CONTENTS

INTRODUCTION

Argentina has always been the odd one out in South America. Taking up practically the entire bottom half of that continent, it is second in size only to Brazil. It includes territories as diverse as the frozen wastes of Tierra del Fuego, the fertile plains of the pampas, subtropical rainforest and the sweeping Atlantic coastline. But it's the people and not just the fabulous geography that makes Argentina such an extraordinary country.

If you choose to stay or seek your fortune in Argentina, you won't be alone. The country is a nation of immigrants who have generated a fiery blend of European sophistication and Latin passion in the heart of South America. The happy result of this blend is that everyone has brought along their own slice of culture, be it dashing British polo or divine Italian pizza. Yet at the same time something unique has emerged in Argentina. You can hear it in the fast *lunfardo* slang spoken on the streets of Buenos Aires, you can see it in the erotic embrace of the tango dancers and you can taste it in the mouth-watering steaks.

Maybe the Argentines' reputation for arrogance is well deserved. After all, when you think of it, they have an awful lot to be arrogant about. Steak and good looks aside, Argentina can boast a share of the world's most spectacular waterfall, the highest mountain this side of the Himalayas and one of the most sophisticated cities on earth. Culturally, it's a dream and continues to churn out writers of extraordinary calibre, cutting-edge cinema, lively theatre and of course the tango. There aren't many other dances in the world that can make the bold claim of being 'the closest thing you'll find to a vertical expression of horizontal desire'.

Argentines are a boisterous lot. If you enjoy being the centre of attention you're in for considerable competition. In the cities, there is a constant background noise of revving engines, screeching brakes, televised football matches and the happy clatter of packed restaurants. This is a nation that loves to talk and will do so loudly at every available opportunity. Spontaneous debates spring up on street corners, in bank queues and on buses. Eavesdroppers will be in heaven.

In Argentina you go out at all hours and you go out to be seen. It is not unusual to finish dinner at midnight or grab breakfast on your way back from an exhausting night on the tiles before heading straight to work. Argentines are certainly not wallflowers, and they won't expect you to be one either. But if you really want to get the most out of your stay in Argentina, you may have to revamp your sleeping habits. This is the perfect place for insomniacs. Whether it's the result of an unrivalled caffeine intake, the simple fact that they can never pass up an opportunity to socialise or sheer willpower alone, Argentines seem to spend less time asleep than other nationalities.

This is also the land of svelte models and ravishing polo players so come fashionably prepared. They are a sophisticated bunch and Buenos Aires has put in a lot of hard work to be known as the Paris of South America. Life in the countryside may be more relaxed and a welcome respite from the frantic city pace, but even here things are done with style.

You have also chosen a relatively safe country, provided you don't get inside a car (Argentines are some of the most aggressive drivers in the world). Forget any preconceived notions about South America. Down here you can eat the salad and drink the tap water. People still walk around the streets at three in the morning—actually they're probably just on their way out to a party. There are no really nasty bugs; few terrorist attacks and even the generals—a key feature in the country's political history—have taken a back seat since the return to democracy in 1983. Meanwhile, the economy, which was so badly hit in the 2001 crisis has, in true Argentine style, bounded back.

Despite its enormous size and European feel, Argentina retains a remarkably intimate atmosphere. Argentines are the most courteous of people and you will always find yourself drawn into conversation. It can be safely said that wherever you come from in the world, no one will raise an eyebrow or call you a gringo straight off. If you're really lucky you may even be stopped and asked directions.

Packed with anecdotes, practical tips and invaluable

information, the following pages will take you through the intricacies of Argentine society and customs and, I hope, make your stay all the more enjoyable.

So take a deep breath because coming to Argentina is like being plunged into the movies with the volume turned up full. Larger-than-life characters frolic through unbelievable scenery, everyone drives at 100 miles an hour and the weekend starts on Wednesday.

ACKNOWLEDGEMENTS

My special thanks go to Jamie Grant for the wonderful photos and everything else. Also enormous thanks to Rodolfo 'Yoyo' de Los Santos, Nico Busch, Santi Norris and Daniela Volker for patiently helping me with hours of research. Thanks as well to Charlie Froggatt for his insights on polo and Katya Lamerton Viegas for long discussions on the tango. I'd also like to thank the 'gang' in San Telmo—Uri, Anim, Diego, Fernando, Chino, Shannen and DJ—for being such lovely flatmates; Federico and Veronica D'Angelo in Ushuaia; Mark Cramer, Dan Buck, Dereck Foster, Richard Cunningham, Joe Oppenheimer and my parents, Jean and Roger, for their support and encouragement. And finally, many thanks to the hundreds of others who have helped along the way and without whom this book would not have been possible.

To my *viejos*,
with love

MAP OF ARGENTINA

BOLIVIA

PARAGUAY

BRAZIL

CHILE

ARGENTINA

URUGUAY

PACIFIC
OCEAN

● BUENOS
AIRES

ATLANTIC
OCEAN

FIRST IMPRESSIONS

CHAPTER 1

'All grass and sky, and sky and grass,
and still more sky and grass.'
—Adventurer and author R.B. Cunninghame Graham,
on Argentina's Pampas

Bᴵ ᴛʜᴇ ᴛɪᴍᴇ ʏᴏᴜʀ ᴛᴀxɪ ᴅʀɪᴠᴇʀ picks you up from Ezeiza airport and weaves through a terrifying maze of traffic lanes with his foot firmly glued to the accelerator, you may start to get some idea of what you've let yourself in for. He is gesticulating wildly—hands waving this way and that like so many windmills—and letting loose a stream of Spanish. It's hard to follow exactly what he is saying as his sentences are peppered with *lunfardo*. He sounds almost Italian but you manage to pick up something about Argentina having the finest beef, the best-looking women (lots of gesticulations here), the greatest footballers and basically being the most marvelous place on Earth. Welcome to Argentina, a country you don't really visit but one that grabs you from the moment your plane touches down in Buenos Aires and doesn't let you go, even after you've long since left.

The first thing that strikes the foreign visitor to Argentina is whether the Argentines are Latin Americans or Europeans who through a strange twist of fate have been uprooted and thrown into the middle of South America. It is a dilemma that continues to confound the Argentines themselves.

A local saying reasons that 'Argentina is the most European of the Latin American nations because its people are from the most Latin of the European nations'. It's certainly true that the vast majority of the population can trace their forefathers back to Europe (mainly Spain and Italy). And Buenos Aires appears to be a city built by some seriously homesick

Europeans. A short walk across this most sophisticated metropolis is like a whirlwind tour of Europe. Glance at a menu and you could think you're in Italy. Mingle with the polo players and you could be in Britain. Go shopping and you might think you're in France. Culturally and emotionally, Argentina remains firmly attached to Europe and its eyes are continually straining across the Atlantic for inspiration and approval.

Occasionally, as the distance from their ideological homeland makes itself felt, the Argentines sink into despair and moan that they feel abandoned by the rest of the world. They say that *porteños*, as the inhabitants of Buenos Aires are better known, are a melancholic lot. Maybe it's the thought of an exile without return—a creeping nostalgia for the countries that they have left behind.

But once you get out of the major cities there is a dramatic return to South American reality. Horse-drawn carts piled with exotic fruits rattle over cobbled streets and men in ponchos and sombreros slip away from the midday heat for long siestas. Ah, you decide, maybe I'm in South America after

Even when there is an occasion for celebration and fun, like in this instance of a carnival taking place in the city of Jujuy, Argentines seldom need to find an excuse to live it up!

A colourful tango bar in
La Boca, Buenos Aires.

all. Then an expensive-looking blonde in a fur coat strides past and you're back to square one.

The city of Buenos Aires is a nation unto itself. It's a monster of a place—tangled and noisy, modern and old with wide, sweeping boulevards, expansive parks and striking architecture. At one moment you are in the swanky financial districts and docklands of London. Two streets down and it's chic Paris where fashion is everything and the beautiful people check you out starting with your shoes. Another block and you're in 19th century Madrid. Grand, now crumbling, facades tell of a time of decadence long past. And what, if anything, holds this strange boiling pot of a city together? Like New York, Buenos Aires is a city of immigrants. It is no one people but a mix of all, drawn here for hundreds of years in search of fame, fortune and a new beginning. Yet Buenos Aires has something beyond its disparate people and parts. You feel it in the cafes, filled with smoke and noise. It's in the passion for football, a whole city fixed to tiny TV screens in the restaurants bars and shops all frantically cheering on their team and baying for the other side's blood. The melancholic music of the tango is the soundtrack to this extraordinary place.

Then there's the other Argentina, the countryside. Drive out from Buenos Aires and you're in the vast grasslands of the Pampas: perfectly flat and an endless horizon of sky and grass. Further south, penguins and whales wallow in the South Atlantic seas while adventurers continue to be drawn by the magical Patagonian plains. Here the majestic Andes rise up to their most extreme heights and glaciers plunge into icy seas. To the North lie the high and arid plains of Salta and the lush subtropical rainforest of Iguazul'.

Argentina is an immense and stunning country, incorporating every possible type of climate, altitude and landscape you can imagine—and a lot more that defies imagination until you've seen it with your own eyes. It won't be long before you realize that you are in a country of extremes whose turbulent history and impassioned peoples compete with the landscape to make this such a wonderful yet extraordinary place.

CHAPTER 2

LAND AND HISTORY

'I must tell you there's scarcely a gaucho left
All round my native parts;
Some are under the grass, and some have fled,
And some in the frontier wars are dead;
For as soon, in this land, as one war is done,
Some other rumpus starts.'
—from The Gaucho Martín Fierro, by José Hernández,
translation by Walter Owen

SHAKY BEGINNINGS

The *Conquistadors*, finding neither silver nor gold in the region that was to become present-day Argentina, nor local indigenous tribes docile enough to exploit, pretty much left the place to its own devices, preferring instead to plunder the great indigenous empires of Central America and Peru. By 1570, less than 2,000 Spaniards lived in the country and Buenos Aires itself was little more than an abandoned settlement.

Today's common expression that *Buenos Aires te mata* (Buenos Aires kills you)—a jokey reference to the oppressive metropolis of 13 million inhabitants and stifling humidity—actually has some historical grains of truth; the earliest visitors to the region didn't fare well to say the least. The first European to explore the River Plate in 1516, Juan Diaz de Solis, a Portuguese navigator employed by the Spanish Crown, was attacked and, legend has it, eaten by the local Querandí tribe. Some 20 years later the aristocrat Pedro de Mendoza set sail from Spain and founded a small encampment, which he christened Santa Maria de Buen Aire after the patron saint of sailors. Besieged by indigenous peoples, Mendoza's 1,600-strong army at one stage resorted to eating the leather off their shoes to avoid starvation. One Spaniard reputedly ate his own brother. By 1541, the settlement was abandoned. Mendoza managed to escape Buenos Aires alive, only to perish of syphilis on the high seas. Meanwhile, some of the livestock that had been brought over by the Spaniards escaped and were left to run wild on the fertile pampas where they bred rapidly. They would soon become the criollo ponies and enormous cattle herds that made Argentina so famous.

It wasn't until 1580 before another Spaniard, Juan de Garay, tried his luck in Buenos Aires. He planted a tree and drew up a plan for the city before being caught unawares as he took a siesta on the banks of the Río de La Plata. The Querandí killed Garay, but this time Buenos Aires survived—an isolated outpost on the fringe of the Spanish empire.

Other Argentine cities including Tucumán, Salta, Jujuy, La Rioja and Córdoba were colonised from the north, by way of silver-rich Potosi in Alto Peru (present-day Bolivia) and Lima, where the Spanish Crown had its viceroyalty. Many beautiful colonial buildings and churches survive intact around central plazas, making such cities some of the most picturesque in the country.

Back in Buenos Aires, the local population indulged in a profitable smuggling racket with the Portuguese and British—much to the irritation of the Spanish Crown who insisted that

Argentines enjoying the evening weather and view of the Casa Rosada Palace on the Plaza de Mayo, which is a place of great historical significance in Argentina's history.

Historical landmarks such as this colonial church in the village of Cachi, Salta can be found throughout the country.

all trade went via their viceroyalty in Lima, Peru. They also traded in the hides and meat of the enormous cattle herds that roamed the pampas, the vast grassy plains that surround Buenos Aires. It was at this time that the legendary gaucho first emerged. Argentina's cowboy began his life as a cattle hustler and an outlaw during the 18th and 19th centuries, fearlessly riding across the pampas on horseback.

It wasn't until 1776, nearly two hundred years after Garay's historic founding of Buenos Aires, that Argentina was finally given its own viceroyalty of the Río de la Plata with its seat in Buenos Aires.

So much for great beginnings. But if Argentina doesn't stand out like Peru or Mexico for the grandeur of its colonial days, it did produce more than its fair share of heroes when the criollos (Spaniards born in Argentina) finally shook off the Spanish Crown at the beginning of the 19th century.

BOOTING OUT THE SPANISH

A number of simultaneous events led to Spain's demise in the Americas, among them the Napoleonic wars in Europe and the increasing discontent of the *criollos* with their Spanish overlords and their infuriating trade laws. In Argentina, things were speeded along by a rather singular event.

In 1806, the Englishman Sir Home Popham decided to invade Buenos Aires completely off his own bat. Popham, presumably still fired up after fighting the Dutch in Cape Town, had neither backing nor authorisation from the British government when he landed in Buenos Aires with a naval and military force of 1,600 men. Rather than standing his ground, the cowardly Spanish viceroy scuttled off to Córdoba, leaving the *porteños* to defend their city, which they did successfully. They ousted the British—not once, but again a year later, when the British government sent a second expedition headed by Lieutenant General John Whitelocke. This unprecedented success boosted *porteño* self-esteem to such an extent that it gave them the added confidence to throw off their Spanish rulers in the revolution of 25 May 1810 and declare an independent junta.

> The real hero of the independence movement was General José de San Martín, the Argentine who later went on to cross the Andes on horseback to liberate Chile and Peru for good measure. He is one of the few historical figures above criticism in Argentina, and the anniversary of his death on 17 August is a national holiday. In almost every town and city in Argentina you will come across a street or plaza named after San Martín, and there is usually also a statue of the hero mounted on a rearing horse.

Independence from Spain was formally proclaimed six years later on 9 July 1816 in the northern city of Tucumán. As a result, Argentina happily enjoys two more public holidays: both 25 May and 9 July are celebrated as national holidays. And both are among Buenos Aires' greatest landmarks. The Plaza de Mayo in front of the Casa Rosada (the presidential palace) commemorates the May Revolution and the giant road bisecting the city and arguably the widest road in the world is christened the Avenida Nueve de Julio (9th of July Avenue).

Independence from the Spanish Crown, however, didn't mean political stability for Argentina. The country remained wracked by political divisions, as provincial warlords competed for control. The most alarming development was the ever-widening chasm between the *porteños* of Buenos Aires and the rest of the country.

Blue and white are Argentina's national colours, as represented on the country's national flag. According to popular interpretation, the blue stripes represent the colour of the Virgin Mary's robes and the white symbolises *argentum* (Latin for silver), from which the name Argentina comes from.

THE GREAT DIVIDE:
BUENOS AIRES AND THE INTERIOR

If a *porteño* tells you that he comes from the north, what he probably means is that he's from the north of Buenos Aires city. The inhabitants of Buenos Aires are enormously proud of their city and at times are apt to believe it is the centre of the universe. The rest of Argentina is simply referred to as 'the Interior'—a somewhat murky and ill-defined description that embraces every possible terrain from Tierra del Fuego in the south to the dusty Bolivian border in the north.

While *porteños* tend to think of themselves as sophisticated creatures, they look upon their fellow countrymen from the Interior as something more akin to country yokels. The striking division between Buenos Aires and the Interior can be traced back to the years just after independence when the country fell into two distinct camps—Unitarists and Federalists—and civil war ensued. The Unitarists, generally cosmopolitan city folk from Buenos Aires with eyes locked lovingly on Europe, believed in a strong central government (in Buenos Aires, of course). The Federalists wanted to preserve local autonomy and soon fell under the tyrannical rule of Juan Manuel de Rosas, the greatest Federalist of them all. (His portrait appears today, rather controversially, on the 20-peso bill. He is easily identifiable by his cruel looking mouth and enormous sideburns.)

Rosas, the gaucho warlord of Buenos Aires province, sought and achieved full dictatorial powers in 1829 and ran the province as he would a vast ranch. When his first term as governor ended, he left Buenos Aires on a military campaign to wipe out bands of 'Indians' in the south, only to return to office in 1835 and rule for another 17 years with the help of an intricate spy network and brutal secret police. During Rosas' reign, you could get into trouble if you didn't wear a red ribbon—the federalist colour—or begin a letter with the slogan 'Long live the Federation and death to the Unitarist savages'. To top it off, he even revived the slave trade for a while. Eventually his enemies—and they were plenty—united against him. Rosas was overthrown in 1852 and fled the country on a British steamer bound for Southampton, where he blew his fortune trying to recreate an Argentine *estancia* in the English countryside.

With Rosas out of the way, Argentina was soon well on track to becoming a nation state. A federal constitution was established in 1853. In 1862, Bartolomé Mitre was sworn in as the first president of the Republic and Buenos Aires city's status was formalised by 1886, when it was made a Federal Capital.

'The history of Buenos Aires is written in its telephone directory,' writes Bruce Chatwin in his now legendary *In Patagonia*. A random selection among the 'Rs' throws up a Romanov, a Rommel, a Radziwil, a Rose and a Rothschild. They're all still there today in addition to an even more exotic roll call as Argentina continues to welcome immigrants from across the globe.

Argentina now faced a dilemma. It had an abundance of glorious fertile land and a miserable lack of people. The country was desperate for cultivation and colonisation.

FROM THE BOATS

The response was massive immigration as Argentina turned to Europe for capital and people. Boats landed at the bustling port of Buenos Aires, and out of them poured immigrants in their droves. Between 1857 and 1924 more than 5.5 million people came to Argentina; over 3 million stayed. The majority came from the Mediterranean countries—half were Italians, a quarter were Spaniards. But immigrants also came from Germany, Britain, Russia, Poland, France and the Middle East. Among them were land speculators, entrepreneurs and romantic adventurers, but mostly they were poor Europeans seeking a better life in the New World. Immigration remained a government priority for the better part of a century and has intrinsically shaped present-day Argentina. By 1914, one-third of the country's population had been born abroad and 80 per cent of the country was either immigrants or their children.

Other Latin Americans are fond of reminding their aloof and arrogant neighbour in the south of its humble beginnings. 'The Bolivians and Peruvians come from the Incas,' they boast. 'The Guatemalans come from the Maya and the Mexicans from the Aztecs. But the Argentines,' they sneer, 'they come from the boats.'

'The truth,' say the Argentines, 'is that the rest of Latin America is plain jealous. We're taller, blonder and richer.'

THE INDIGENOUS PEOPLE

The fact that the Argentines are on the whole taller and fairer than their Latin American neighbours remains a sensitive subject—Argentina's indigenous population was quickly and ruthlessly obliterated. There was practically no chance for the native people to mix with their European counterparts to create a dominant *mestizo* race that is so characteristic of Mexico and other Latin American nations.

Indigenous communities in pre-Conquest Argentina never reached anywhere near the enormous numbers found in Central America and Peru. Historian David Rock estimates that at the time of the Conquest they numbered no more than between 750,000 and quite possibly half that number. With only two people for every three square miles, many lived as nomadic hunters and gatherers. Tribes such as the Querandí roamed the pampas, where they would hunt rheas (a type of ostrich) and guanacos (a type of llama) with *boleadoras* (weighted three-thonged lassos). In the far south, the Yamana Indians speared seals and fish and travelled in canoes. More organised and sedentary groups such as the Diaguita inhabited the north of the country. But north and south, all of them were vulnerable. Those that survived the Spanish Conquest and its aftermath were later slaughtered during the state-sponsored 'desert campaigns' of the 19th century. At one stage during this particularly gruesome chapter of Argentina's history, local landowners offered a gold sovereign for each 'Indian' ear.

Today, remaining indigenous groups form less than 2 per cent of the total population (some estimates are as low as 0.5 per cent), while *mestizos* (people with mixed European and Indian ancestry) account for less than 15 per cent. Most of these indigenous communities are found in the far north of the country on the Paraguayan, Bolivian and Brazilian borders. The largest groups are the Quechua, Toba, Wichi and Guaraní but there are also isolated groups of Mapuche and Tehuelche Indians still living in Patagonia.

Many live in conditions of extreme poverty on the fringes of Argentine society and fight a constant battle to uphold their cultural identity and rights in a country where the expression *Que Indio* is still used to describe a barbarian and people go out of their way to point out that they are from 'good European stock' and have no 'Indian' blood.

THE PERÓNS

With the coming of the immigrants, Argentina entered an astonishing period of growth and prosperity, to emerge the world's sixth richest nation. In France they even had a saying, *riche comme un Argentin*, thanks to the extravagantly wealthy Argentines who holidayed in Paris. But the country's money remained in the hands of the oligarchy and *estancieros* (large landowners), many of whom lived on *estancias* (ranches) the size of small kingdoms. Few of the immigrants ever made it out of the cities and by the early 20th century an increasingly militant and urban working class began clamouring for social change. It was to these dissatisfied masses that Juan Domingo Perón appealed.

Few names from Argentina's turbulent past still conjure up such emotion as that of Perón, both General Juan Domingo Perón and his charismatic wife Evita. Perón came to prominence on the back of a military coup in 1943 and was soon made head of the labour ministry, where he built up a powerful base among the trade unions and urban working class. He married Evita, his glamorous mistress and an aspiring actress, in a secret ceremony a few months before he was elected president in 1946. He remained president until 1955. Together, the Peróns promised a 'New Argentina' founded on social justice and economic independence. They didn't make much of an attempt to hide their hatred for the upper classes. Evita once declared that "There are two things of which I am proud: my love for the people and my hatred for the oligarchy." Not to be outdone by his wife's idealism, Perón had the Jockey Club—the bastion of the upper classes in Buenos Aires—burnt down.

Argentina remains divided on the issue of the Peróns to this day. Perón's supporters—known as *peronistas*—argue that Perón's administration brought about striking social reforms including the introduction of state pensions, workers' rights and full legal status for the trade unions. Members of the Justicialist Party (the formal name given to the Peronist political party) still chant Perón's name and march beneath banners of Evita's face. Anti-*peronistas* brand Perón a dictator, drawing attention to his Nazi ties and secret bank accounts, and holding him accountable for the economic ruin of the country.

In 1955, Perón was ousted by yet another military coup. He fled first to Paraguay and later to Spain, where he lived in stately exile for the next 17 years, finally returning to Argentina in 1973.

Newly elected president Juan Perón gives an oath in front of the Senate and Chamber in Buenos Aires, 1946.

Don't Cry For Me, Argentina'

Depending on whether or not you're a *peronista*, Evita is either a saint or a sinner—there is no middle ground. As the illegitimate child of Juan Duarte and Juana Ibarguren, Evita's beginnings were remarkably humble. She grew up in a small dreary town in the pampas, living with four brothers and sisters in a modest house that her mother ran as a *pensión*. At the tender age of 15, she left for Buenos Aires with a tango singer, hoping to make it as an actress. But for years she barely scraped by. Half starved, she would act for just a cup of milky coffee. Eventually she made it as a radio actress but her ignominious beginnings and illegitimacy always hung over her.

Even as the president's wife, Argentina's elite consistently snubbed Evita. The ultimate affront came when the aristocratic ladies of Buenos Aires society refused to grant her the presidency of the Benevolent Ladies Trust charity, an honour traditionally given to all of Argentina's First Ladies. Not one to take a back seat in life, Evita dyed her hair blonde, dressed in Dior, shut down the Benevolent Ladies and set up her own charity, the Eva Perón Foundation. Swarms of the poor flocked to the foundation's office in the labour ministry, where Evita directed the construction of hundreds of hospitals, schools and clinics across the country and in moments of abandon handed out 100 peso notes, bicycles, sewing machines and false teeth to her shirtless ones or *descamisados* as she called them. They called her—and still call her—the Spiritual Chief of the Nation, Lady of Hope, Leader of the Humble and even Saint Evita.

When she died of uterine cancer in 1952 at the age of 33, forty thousand Argentines wrote to the Pope to demand her immediate canonisation. Half a million mourners queued for hours to kiss her coffin and some people even tried to commit suicide around her body as it lay in state. The country remained in mourning for weeks.

But Evita's power did not die with her. Her face, whether that of the angry woman clutching a microphone or the young, smiling, airbrushed blonde, is regularly used on *peronista* campaign posters today and appears framed on the walls of *peronista* households throughout the country. Her nuclear-proof tomb in Recoleta cemetery is now one of the country's top tourist attractions. When Alan Parker's film *Evita* was released in 1997, it was bound to cause controversy. Once again, a lavishly dressed blonde leant over the balcony of the Casa Rosada, only this time it was Madonna. As you can well guess, this infuriated the country's *peronistas*. Here was Madonna, a racy pop star, not to mention a *yankee*, playing the role of their beloved Evita. The matter wasn't helped by the fact that the script hinted that their spiritual leader had slept her way to the top. The vice-president (a *peronista*) urged people to boycott the film, two cinemas showing Evita were smoke-bombed and a professional wrestler challenged Parker to a duel with the director's weapon of choice.

The fact that half a century since her death, Evita can still provoke such turmoil speaks for itself. Her legend, like the embalmed body lying in Recoleta cemetery, is indestructible.

Evita Perón—saint or sinner?

THE DIRTY WAR

Although Perón did not return to Argentina until 1973, throughout his years of exile *peronismo*—the force behind Perón—remained a major feature in Argentina. Governments came and went but none came anywhere near the popularity that Perón had achieved in the 1940s and 1950s. By the early 1970s pro-*peronista* guerrilla groups had started to emerge. They staged regular high-profile kidnappings and bank robberies and the country steadily plunged into chaos and anarchy. Perón's return to Argentina in 1973 seemed like an obvious solution and he was promptly elected president with 60 per cent of the vote. Less than a year into his presidency, Perón died and Argentina was left under the control of his third and largely incompetent wife, Isabelita, a former nightclub dancer whom he had met in Panama. As you can imagine, it didn't take long for the generals to step in again and form a ruling military junta under General Jorge Videla.

What happened next is undoubtedly the blackest chapter of Argentina's recent history and remains an open wound in Argentina's conscience. From 1976 until 1983, Argentina remained under the control of a series of military juntas. During this period, chillingly dubbed *El Proceso* (the Process), the armed forces waged a bloody and indiscriminate 'Dirty War' against thousands of supposed 'subversives'.

The guerrilla groups, which had been active since 1970, were the military's primary targets. These were comprised of mainly young professionals and students, often with affluent middle-class backgrounds. Most were in their 20s and there were large numbers of young female combatants. The military's reprisals were far worse than anything the leftist guerrilla groups had carried out. While the guerrillas may have killed 200–300 people at the most, *El Proceso* claimed the lives of tens of thousands of Argentines. Human rights groups estimate that as many as 30,000 people were killed or 'disappeared' during this time.

No one was above suspicion and thousands of Argentines were taken from their homes, rounded up and sent to clandestine torture centres across the country. Victims included trade unionists, socialists, psychologists, human rights and other activists, nuns, priests, pacifists, journalists, teachers, lawyers, doctors, students, children, pensioners and housewives. They were bundled into Ford Falcons and driven off by men in dark glasses, never to be seen again. (Even today, 20 years later, the sight of a Ford Falcon can send a shiver down many a spine.)

The military government repeatedly denied the existence of the torture centres and of the prisoners held there. With no official status, the prisoners did not exist—they had 'disappeared'. All the prisoners were, without exception, systematically tortured. The torturers were after names and addresses of dissidents allegedly involved in subversive activities. But more often than not, the victims were innocent bystanders caught up in the witch-hunt—they had no names to give.

Inside the torture centres, prisoners were submitted to electric shocks, continual beatings and mock executions. Some were buried up to their necks in the ground and left there for days. Others were forced to witness the torture of their own families. Then finally, when no more could be done with them, they were thrown from planes into the Río de la Plata—many of them drugged and still alive.

Ironically, it was the war against Britain over the Falklands/ Malvinas Islands in 1982 that brought about the end of military rule in Argentina. The military's ignominious defeat by crack British troops and the capture of 10,000 Argentine soldiers further discredited a military government that was also facing economic ruin and increasing pressure from the families of the 'disappeared'. General Leopoldo Galtieri, who headed the military junta at that time, was promptly booted out of the Casa Rosada, and millions of exuberant Argentines greeted the subsequent return to democracy in 1983.

KEY POLITICAL ISSUES

With democracy once again restored in Argentina, the government returned to the principles of the 1853 constitution. This was revised in 1994 with 19 new articles, 40 amendments and an additional chapter on New Rights and Guarantees. Argentina has more than 20 political parties. The two largest are the peronist Justicialist Party (Partido Justicialista or PJ) and the more moderate Radical Civic Union (Unión Cívica Radical or UCR). Since the 1990s the centre-left Frente por un Pais Solidario (Frepaso) has emerged as a serious contender for the PJ.

As the first democratically elected president since the return to civilian rule in 1983, President Raúl Alfonsín from the UCR was faced with the delicate task of dealing with the military. He put former junta members on trial and several high-ranking military officials were jailed for crimes against humanity committed during the Dirty War. But under

Silhouettes demarcated on the grounds of the Plaza de Mayo represent the Argentines who disappeared during the 'Dirty War'.

increasing pressure and a threatened military uprising in 1987, Alfonsín was eventually forced to concede. He passed two controversial laws that absolved lower-ranking military officers from crimes on the grounds that they were simply acting under orders and put a moratorium on all trials. When President Carlos Menem of the PJ won the 1989 election, he surprised the nation further when he pardoned and released General Jorge Videla and other military officers from jail. With the arrival of Néstor Kirchner to the presidency in 2003, perpetrators of the Dirty War are once again facing charges for kidnapping and murder.

Ownership of the Falkland Islands, known as Las Islas Malvinas in Argentina, continues to be a bone of contention, with successive governments pledging their return to Argentina. But the biggest challenge facing Argentina's leaders since the country's return to democracy is getting the shambolic economy back on to a stronger footing.

THE ECONOMIC SITUATION

Argentina is fabulously rich in natural resources and has a highly educated and skilled workforce of over 15 million.

As much as 88 per cent of the country is urban and a third of the population live in greater Buenos Aires, making this the economic as well as the political hub of the country. Fanning out from Buenos Aires is the pampas

High Inflation

Argentina is the only country in the world to have suffered more than 15 years of continuous triple-digit inflation. By 1989, inflation had reached an annual level of over 4,000 per cent.

—expansive fertile grasslands that are justly famous for producing top-quality wheat and cattle. Sugar and tobacco thrive in the north, and the south is home to vast sheep stations and rich supplies of largely untapped minerals. Argentina is also self-sufficient in petroleum and other energy resources.

Agriculture and agro-industry remain of major importance in Argentina's economy. However, manufacturing of iron, steel, cars, textiles, industrial chemicals, machinery, transport equipment and hydroelectric power is also important. The country's trade unions remain well developed and independent, although they do not hold the massive political clout they once did under Perón.

All this seems like the perfect scenario for a booming economy, and indeed Argentina is one of Latin America's wealthiest countries. Yet years of political chaos, military intervention and ineffectual civilian rule have meant that Argentina's economy has never managed to fulfil its vast potential. A leading question that still confounds observers today is 'what went wrong?' Why was one of the richest countries in the world in 1914, exporting half the world's beef and much of its wheat and grain supplies, been burdened by unemployment, poverty, crippling foreign debt and spiralling inflation?

Initial attempts by President Alfonsín to curb inflation failed and it was the maverick President Menem who, on coming to power in 1989 on a populist campaign, introduced a wide-sweeping privatisation plan and reduced trade barriers. Argentina's telephone company, airlines, most railways, electric power generation companies, national oil company, steel mills, ports, airports, TV stations and most public services were transferred to the private sector. In 1991, his administration pegged the Argentine peso to the US dollar with the convertibility law thus curbing hyperinflation and stabilizing the economy. But as Menem's presidency drew towards the end of its second term it became increasingly criticized for being frivolous and corrupt. His neo-liberal policies resulted in massive layoffs, rising unemployment, an increasingly high cost of living for most Argentines and crippling foreign debt. In 1999, the incoming president Fernando de la Rua inherited a US$ 114 billion foreign debt and an economy in dire straits. By 2000, Argentina was in deep recession, unemployment was soaring (it would eventually reach above 20 per cent) and the country had come to the

Sheep farming makes up a major component of Argentina's economy.

end of its tether. With their faith in the economy rapidly failing, Argentines started to remove their savings from the banks, resulting in the highly unpopular *corralito* in which the government effectively froze bank accounts. For the Argentines, this was a step too far and they started to take to the streets banging pots and pans in protest. By the end of 2001 the protests (known as the *cacerolazo*) had become a nightly occurrence and were turning increasing violent. On 21 December, clashes with the police left 27 demonstrators dead. President de la Rua had no option but to resign, fleeing the Casa Rosada in a helicopter. The ensuing ten days saw a series of presidents come and go until Eduardo Duhalde was appointed interim President. Duhalde had no option but to default on the country's foreign debt and abandon the peso's pegging to the dollar, causing it to devalue sharply. Millions of Argentines lost their life savings overnight. Over half the country plunged below the poverty line and soup kitchens and barter markets became commonplace.

Argentina officially came out of its recession in 2003 and since then Argentina is enjoying a period of high economic growth and relative political stability. GDP for the last three years has been up on average between 8–9 per cent. Unemployment is down to about 10 per cent although inflation, presently hovering at about 10 per cent, continues to be an issue,

THE COUNTRY

Argentina is the eighth largest country in the world and the second largest in South America after Brazil. For administrative purposes it is divided into 23 provinces and the city of Buenos Aires, which is classified as a federal district. The physical characteristics vary tremendously between the provinces and even within each province. The country's main geographic features, however, range from the dense subtropical forests of the north to the Andes mountains in the west and the vast grassy plains of the pampas that fan out from Buenos Aires down into the Patagonian plateaux of the south. *'Gracias a la vida'*—'Thank you life,' sings Mercedes Sosa, Argentina's much-loved folk singer, in her deep voice. 'You've given me so much; cities and lakes, beaches and deserts, mountains and plains.' You can see her point exactly.

As if this geographical mosaic isn't enough, Argentina also lays claim to the Falkland Islands, known locally as Las Islas Malvinas, as well as the more obscure Shag and Black Rocks, South Georgia, the South Sandwich Islands, the South Shetland Islands, the South Orkney Islands and a considerable slice of Antarctica. Although such territorial claims are internationally disputed, it's illegal to print a map in Argentina stating anything otherwise.

Despite the fact that Argentines are said to hanker after all things European and North American, they are incredibly proud of their own country and will profess to know everything about each place even if they haven't been there themselves. If you enjoy solitude and crowd-free places don't take their travel advice too seriously. Argentines are social creatures by habit and love to go where the action (and everybody else) is. During the summer vacations over January and February, thousands of holiday-makers flock to the seaside towns on the Atlantic coast, briefly swelling the ranks of these small coastal cities to millions.

It won't take you long to discover that there are two Argentinas: Buenos Aires and the rest of the country simply referred to as 'the Interior'. For visitor and native alike, they are worlds apart. A sheep farmer from Santa Cruz province in Argentina's deep south will be just as disoriented in Buenos Aires as a sophisticated *porteño* suddenly finding himself on a Patagonian estancia. The beauty of this setup, however, is that you can skip between cosmopolitan chic and the infinite diversity of the countryside.

BUENOS AIRES

Given this tantalising choice, it seems surprising that more than a third of the country's population have chosen to live in Buenos Aires or its suburbs. Argentina's capital is a powerful magnet that continuously draws Argentines from the provinces and other Latin Americans from neighbouring countries. It is the country's political, economic and social hub, and most of the people who live there wouldn't have it any other way. (A plan in 1986 to move the capital to the Patagonian city of Viedma was greeted with such screams of horror by the *porteños* that it had to be smartly dropped.)

The downside of this human condensation is smouldering pollution and unrelenting noise levels that defy all human experience. Pollution and noise, however, will soon be forgiven as you enjoy being in one of the world's most sophisticated cities, one that justly deserves its nickname, 'the Paris of South America'. The natives of Buenos Aires, the *porteños* (people of the port), have an almost religious fanaticism about their beloved city. 'To me it is a fairy tale that Buenos Aires was founded,' wrote Jorge Luis Borges, one of the most famous *porteños* of all. 'It seems as eternal as water and air.'

The first thing you must get to grips with, should you choose Buenos Aires for your home, is that *porteños* defy all sensible laws of sleep. They appear to survive on a diet of endless coffee and catnaps, interspersed with a frenzied social life. Maybe it's thanks to a Latin temperament or the fact that they can't bear to miss out on a social gathering—in Buenos Aires there's always something going on somewhere—that *porteños* are up all hours of the day and night.

Buenos Aires really comes awake at night. Restaurants, cafés and fabulously stacked bookstalls don't close up just because the sun's gone down. Then of course there are the discos, some with capacity for several thousand, where the sleek and glamorous congregate for hours of endless partying. And don't miss out on the tango bars where couples cling to each other passionately into the small hours of the morning. For the novice, and even for *porteños* themselves, this pace of life is exhausting. 'Buenos Aires kills you,' *porteño* friends tell me. 'But there's no way we would dream of living anywhere else.'

THE INTERIOR

Argentina's Interior has a thoroughly South American feel to it, and just a few hours' drive from downtown Buenos Aires you'll be mingling with modern-day gauchos and enormous herds of horned cattle and enjoying magnificent unpolluted sunsets. There's even time for that great stress buster, the siesta.

Generally, the further south you travel from Buenos Aires, the colder and more desolate it gets, until you arrive in Tierra del Fuego and its capital Ushuaia, which makes the bold—and cold—claim to be the southernmost city in the world. Apart from a cluster of sparsely populated and unforgiving islands, you can go no further south (unless a trip to Antarctica is on your itinerary).

Heading north from Buenos Aires, you start to shed your clothes as a blissful subtropical climate kicks in and lush grassy plains give way to thick forests and vast muddy rivers filled with toucans and caimans (the crocodile's South American cousin). Westward, the Andes mountain chain swells to awesome peaks, creating an almost impenetrable barrier between Argentina and Chile. Eastward lie the Atlantic Ocean and 5,000 km of coastline and windswept beaches.

These are Argentina's natural boundaries, yet you're hardly likely to feel penned in or wanting to leave. Driving the 3,500 km from the Bolivian border in the north to Ushuaia in the far south could take you weeks.

For ease, Argentina's mainland territory of 2.8 million square kilometres can be divided into four major geographic regions: the central pampas, the Andes to the west, the fertile lowland north and Patagonia in the south.

The Pampas

This vast sweeping grassland plain fans out westward from Buenos Aires, running for more than a thousand miles from the Atlantic Ocean to the foothills of the Andes and stretching from the Gran Chaco region in the north to the Río Colorado in the south.

For many, Argentina *is* the pampas. Flat as a billiard table, this is ideal terrain for crops and livestock. Cattle are clearly in heaven here, grazing upon acres of lush grasses—no wonder they so generously provide us with such succulent steaks. The flat horizon of the pampas is broken only by the buildings of an occasional *estancia* surrounded by weeping willows, eucalyptus groves, stately poplars and twisted ombú trees—emerging like islands in a sea of grass and sky. Geographically, its flatness may seem uninteresting, yet the pampas has its own magic —sunsets and sunrises that will knock your socks off and a mean wind that periodically whips itself up into the terrifyingly boisterous *pampero*.

The Andes

Forming the backbone of South America, the Andes run down the entire length of Argentina along its border with Chile, reaching some of their highest peaks. It is in the province of San Juan that the awesome Mount Aconcagua rises to a breathtaking 6,960 metres. In the northern provinces of Salta, La Rioja, San Juan and Mendoza, the foothills of the Andes are filled with vineyards. In the southern province of Neuquén and the western parts of Río Negro, Chubut and Santa Cruz, they become glacial lakes and giant ice fields.

This is the side of Argentina you want to get near if you enjoy adventure sports—skiing, climbing, white-water rafting or just straightforward walking. Hugging the Andes

Those who have a taste for adventure can go white-water rafting, which is one of the many outdoor activities available in San Juan.

from north to south is the famous Route 40, which crosses through scrubby deserts of fat-fingered cacti and the Lake District into Patagonia. With only a third asphalted, Route 40 is the ideal adventure for off-roaders.

The North

In the north of the country, heading eastward from the Andes, the dry mountainous landscape of Salta and Jujuy gives way to the hot scrubby plains of the Gran Chaco —an enormous area that stretches into Paraguay and parts of Brazil and Bolivia. The Chaco engulfs the two Argentine provinces of Chaco and Formosa. Much of this region is completely inaccessible and the western part of Chaco province, a vast uninhabited area, is dubbed El Impenetrable.

Further east still, you cross the Paraná River and enter the provinces of Entre Ríos, Corrientes and Misiones, an area known as Mesopotamia. Bordered on one side by the Paraná and on the other by the River Uruguay, the area has traditionally felt cut off from the rest of the country, but the fertile terrain has made it an important livestock and agricultural centre and great fishing country.

Misiones, the northeasternmost point of Argentina, rises like an isthmus squeezed between Paraguay and Brazil. Here you have the spectacular Iguazú Falls, set in 55,000 hectares of national parkland and subtropical forests. The falls can be viewed from both the Argentine and Brazilian sides, but as the local saying goes, 'The Brazilian side may have the best views but we put on the show.' If it looks familiar, that's because it played the grisly backdrop to the opening scenes of Roland Joffe's 1986 epic film *The Mission*. The area had been the centre of Jesuit activity, where the local Guaraní Indians were placed in *reducciónes* (specially designed communities). Many of the ruins are still visible today.

Patagonia

If any name has the ability to bewitch, surely it must be that of Patagonia. This strange land begins at the Colorado River at 39°S and rolls on down through pastoral steppe and glacial fields to the Magellan Straits at the southernmost tip of the continent. It is sparsely populated, practically treeless and internationally famous for its wind. 'Patagonia without wind,' goes a local saying, 'would be like hell without the devil.'

Early explorers claimed that Patagonia was inhabited by naked giants and monsters. Latter-day travel writer Bruce Chatwin remembers Patagonia from his school days as the safest place to be in the event of a nuclear attack. And lately it has also been getting a reputation

Twisted and bent by fierce winds, the occasional tree relieves the barren Patagonian landscape.

A picturesque view of Monte Fitz Roy and Sucia lagoon in the Los Glaciares National Park in Patagonia.

for dinosaurs, which are being unearthed at an alarming rate from Patagonia's arid plains. Discoveries include the 8-ton predator Giganotosaurus, which makes T. Rex look like his little brother in comparison, and the 100-ton plant-eating Argentinosaurus—the biggest herbivore discovered to date.

Patagonia has also harboured many an outlaw in its past, including the famous North American bandit duo, Butch Cassidy and the Sundance Kid, but today Patagonia also belongs to the rich and famous of the world. Estancia owners are purported to include CNN's Ted Turner, billionaire businessman George Soros, the actor Sylvester Stallone, Italian fashion magnate Luciano Benetton, restaurateur Charlie Lewis and actor Christopher Lambert, all of whom rub shoulders with the locals and an awful lot of sheep.

THE PEOPLE

CHAPTER 3

'What exists here is a ludicrous form of nationalism.
Our entire country is imported. Everybody here is
really from somewhere else.'
—Jorge Luis Borges

AN IDENTITY PROBLEM?

A wit once defined the Argentines as a nation of Italians who speak Spanish, dress as though they're French and like to think they're British. If only it were that simple. Certainly there are millions of descendants of Italians and Spaniards in Argentina. But some in Patagonia speak Welsh and celebrate the *eisteddfod*. Residents of a village in the mountains of Córdoba don *lederhosen* every October for a German beerfest. Buenos Aires boasts the second largest Jewish community outside of Israel (after New York). Sheep farmers in Patagonia still trace their names and sparkling blue eyes back to England, Ireland and Scotland. There are considerable numbers of immigrants from the Middle East, Japan and Asia. The list could go on indefinitely.

The happy result is an exotic mix of customs and cultures and a huge variety of accents and mannerisms here in the heart of South America. Everyone knows where they originally came from and will be eager to tell you about their antecedents. Yet at the same time they are all fiercely proud to be Argentines.

Critics are prone to argue that this cultural melting pot means many Argentines are painfully insecure. At times, Argentines themselves complain bitterly that they suffer a complete lack of national identity. An identity crisis would be understandable. They may live in South America's second largest territory, but there is scarcely a trace of native indigenous blood among them. Less than 2 per cent of the population can call themselves indigenous, while the vast majority originally came from Europe, thousands of miles away and in another hemisphere. Add to that a penchant for bottled blonde, one of the world's highest rates of plastic surgery and an addiction to psychoanalysis, and no wonder they appear to be such an enigma.

But are the Argentines really that elusive? Many would disagree. Once you have met them, they are an easily identifiable race, not least by their distinctive accents, notorious good looks, compulsive *mate* drinking and charming, if at times infuriating, arrogance. 'Abroad, you can recognize an Argentine family a mile off,' says the contemporary Argentine writer Tomás Eloy Martínez. 'Dad in his brown moccasins, the mother's flaming blonde hair … the gesticulations, everything betrays us.'

SERIOUS ATTITUDE

A popular South American joke, one told enthusiastically by the Argentines themselves, asks, 'What's the best bargain in the world?' The answer: 'Buy an Argentine for what he's worth and sell him for what he thinks he's worth.' Arrogance and a generous dosage of vanity—among both men and women—is an accepted fact of life in Argentina. And why not? They are frequently voted the world's best-looking citizens and I've known men to practically fall over backwards after getting an eyeful of the women in Buenos Aires. No one bats an eyelid if you stop and comb your hair in a reflective surface on the street or casually admire your reflection in a spoon in a restaurant. All the elevators have mirrors, hairdressers and beauty parlors do a roaring trade and at times the whiff of aftershave in nightclubs is quite overpowering. Appearance is everything and it's a rare sight to come across an untidy or unkempt Argentine.

Along with this impossible style and good looks, the Argentine possesses a formidable attitude. No smoking signs, if put up in the first place, are religiously ignored and queues were made to be jumped. Although far from rude, Argentines are not known for their reserved character and

TRIGG

won't hesitate to express their opinions, be they political or otherwise. (For this reason, unsuspecting foreigners occasionally dub Argentines 'argy-bargies'.) I once observed an elegantly dressed man gaily gouging out the eyes of smiling politicians from peronist political campaign posters on the street as if it was the most natural thing in the world.

'When you walk into a room you can feel the energy of the Argentines,' an exasperated Uruguayan friend living in Buenos Aires once told me. 'They think that they are number one, that there's nothing or no one above them except God.'

This inflated opinion of themselves gives rise to countless other jibes against Argentines, usually recounted with great relish by other Latin Americans. 'How does an Argentine commit suicide? He throws himself off his own ego!' And have you heard the one about the psychoanalyst who asks his colleague to come over immediately as he has an Argentine on his couch with the strangest affliction. 'So?' says his colleague, 'you see lots of Argentines.' 'Yes,' says the psychoanalyst, 'but this one's got an inferiority complex!'

The following anecdote may put it better. A German acquaintance was on an Aerolineas Argentinas flight from Buenos Aires to Santiago de Chile. The aeroplane had landed and come to a standstill at the airport but the doors remained firmly locked. After a few minutes of confusion she was amused to hear the pilot announce over the tannoy that no one would be allowed to disembark until all of the airline's blankets had been returned to the cabin crew. The passengers, mostly Argentines, eventually stood up and casually pulled out the offending articles from their hand luggage which had been neatly tucked away in the overhead lockers. They weren't embarrassed in the least at being caught red-handed pilfering airline property. The German, new to South America, was momentarily astounded. Later, she found out that she had just witnessed *viveza criolla*—an infamous Argentine attribute—in mass action.

Viveza Criolla and the Vivos

Viveza criolla has been described as anything from 'native cunning' to 'artful lying'. It is a peculiar trait that is both admired and despised, yet it is always carried out in such a charming manner that you simply have to forgive the perpetrator. The man or woman with *viveza criolla* is utterly on the ball, unbelievably quick off the mark in any given situation and always comes out on top. They are known as *vivos*. A good definition of a *vivo* would be that of a man who goes into a revolving door after you but comes out first.

All Argentines, but especially *porteños*, are *vivos* to some extent. The most famous Argentine *vivo* that springs to mind is the footballer Diego Maradona, who rose to the top with the help of both wit and skills. His own brand of *viveza criolla* allowed him to score a winning goal with his hand—or the 'hand of God', as he was quick to point out in a post-match interview—and go on to clinch the 1986 World Cup in Mexico. Unlike the passengers on that Aerolineas Argentinas flight, he got away with cheating, and as far as *viveza criolla* is concerned, it's the getting away with it that matters.

Having said this, you don't need to go around worrying that you will be constantly ripped off in Argentina. Most Argentines are very honest and have an enormous amount of respect for each other and visitors to the country. People will go out of their way to be helpful and spontaneous acts of generosity—known as *gauchadas*—may surprise you. For every act of *viveza criolla* there will always be a *gauchada* to counteract it.

MACHISMO

In Latin America there's no getting away from machismo—even in this most European of Latin nations. This fierce and often self-destructive mixture of pride and toughness can be seen in everything from the way the men walk—swaggering and proud—to never showing fear, never losing face and never giving in. But Argentine machismo is probably less marked than the Mexican variety. Argentine men, according to my *porteño* friends, are charming and courteous, even if they can be sexist at times. 'It's nice for a change to have doors opened for you,' is the general consensus among female foreigners in Argentina. (In Argentina a man will probably also stand back and allow a woman to step out of the elevator first, give up his seat for a pregnant or elderly woman, buy dinner for his date, walk nearer the street on a pavement to protect his female companion from traffic and pay for her bus ticket).

Argentine men make charming if not modest Romeos, and eyeing up girls is a national pastime. It is considered a matter of macho honour to murmur comments at passing women on the street. Such comments, known as *piropos*, are an accepted fact of life and are usually politely ignored. Some men come up with rather eloquent compliments such as 'What's going on in Heaven that the angels have come down to Earth?' They may infuriate feminists but are so much part of Argentine society that I have known women to feel offended if they walk one block without anyone making a comment.

Machismo, however, may be expressed in rather less attractive ways to the fairer sex. Comments on women drivers can be maddening. Once, while boarding a bus whose driver was a woman (practically unheard of), I overheard the man boarding before me saying, 'Good God! How dangerous' before his companion merrily chipped in, 'Why aren't you at home with the kids, darling?'

A statue of a naked male torso in downtown Buenos Aires.

But hold on a minute. The Argentine male may be turning into a 'New Man'. Recent surveys have shown that more than ever he now goes to the supermarket, looks after the kids and helps out with housework.

GAUCHOS

Someone who wouldn't dream of going to the supermarket is the gaucho, Argentina's answer to the rough, tough American cowboy and the ultimate Argentine *macho*.

The gaucho, and the romance that surrounds him, is one of the strongest symbols of *argentinidad*—Argentina's precarious national identity. He is considered nothing less than a national hero and his antics both on and off his beloved horse are much admired throughout the country. Sadly, the original gaucho is no more. Sheep farming and the introduction of barbed wire along with the concept of private property at the end of the 19th century put an end to his free-riding existence on the open pampas, where he would ride for days in any direction and kill a cow whenever he was hungry.

The gaucho's possessions were few; he owned not much more than his poncho, saddle and horse. His favoured weapon was the *facón*, a lethally sharp curved knife, which he stuck down the back of his *bombachas* (baggy trousers). He would be equally swift to whip out his *facón* to slit his enemy's throat or to cut off a slice of beef and dexterously pop it into his mouth—where one slip would mean no tongue.

Yet the legacy of the gaucho is still felt today—not least in the superb horsemanship that practically every Argentine who grows up in the countryside seems to be born with. Many insist that the gaucho is still very much alive and well, just in a more modern mould.

Who was this man that Argentines hold in such high esteem? By all accounts the gaucho was a bloodthirsty, fearless and thoroughly anarchistic individual who answered to no one and would only resort to paid work to keep himself in supplies of rum, tobacco and *yerba mate*—a mildly addictive green tea which helps suppress the appetite and on which he was hooked. It was a lifestyle rather than genes that defined the gaucho. He could be indigenous, a runaway slave, a *mestizo* or a European. As the 20th century writer Adolfo Bioy Casares pointed out, one of the 'gauchos most gaucho' he had known was a French immigrant called Cipriano Cross.

The wide-open pampas was the gaucho's playground where Argentina's famous cattle herds provided an endless source of food. Here he would hunt on horseback, fearlessly whirling *boleadoras* to immobilize his prey, which could be anything from small birds and ostriches to fully-grown cattle. Nothing fazed him except perhaps losing his horse—the real love of his life. This short *gauchesco* verse puts it more succinctly:

A gaucho showing everyone his skill for breaking in horses in San Antonio, a settlement located a few hundred kilometres from Buenos Aires.

My wife and my horse have gone to Salta.
My wife can stay but I miss my horse.

A gaucho without a horse was like a man without legs. The horse not only shaped his lifestyle but changed him physically as well. Off his horse, the gaucho was transformed into a lumbering, bow-legged, stooped being. Everything feasible was done on horseback—to be given unmounted work was considered an insult. There are even eyewitness accounts of a gaucho corpse so molded to the saddle on his horse that he rode to his own funeral.

'His qualities, real and imagined, represent an essential ingredient in the continuous quest by Argentines to define the essence of their national character,' writes Richard W. Slatta, in the gaucho classic, *Gauchos and the Vanishing Frontier*.

The Modern-day Gaucho

Once you get out into the countryside or visit an *estancia* you will invariably come across men who to all intents and purposes look and behave exactly like these gauchos of old. As you watch them galloping across the plains, effortlessly breaking in horses, lassoing cattle and leaping on and off their mounts, it is obvious that these skills have been passed down from generations of experience. After work they may settle down to drink *mate* and later tuck into huge slabs of meat that have been slowly roasted over an open fire, or slip off to the local *pulpería* (a general store that doubles up as a tavern) to drink, indulge in a little gambling and sing along to the guitar. Many continue to wear the trademark baggy *bombacha* trousers tucked into calfskin boots with a red scarf tied around their neck and a *rastra* (a heavy leather belt decorated with silver coins) around their waist. If you look closely you'll probably be able to spot a *facón* tucked down their waistband. These men may be referred to as *peónes* or ranch hands, but more often than not they are simply called gauchos.

DRIVERS

In the city, the motorcar has replaced the horse. Driving is insane and there is much scope for expressing machismo on the roads. 'The Argentine driver is a dangerous driver,' complained a member of the Argentine Automobile Club. 'Sure, he's capable enough but he acts as if he's the only one on the road.'

Within hours of your arrival, you will already have gathered that anything goes. Overtaking on the inside, chatting on mobile phones, shooting red lights and not wearing a seatbelt may be illegal but are all pars for the course. It also seems to be a matter of honour to let rip a torrent of abuse at passing motorists who are driving just as badly as you are and to rev your engine to scare the wits out of pedestrians at crossings.

In addition to an unhealthy love of speed, Argentine drivers may drive with no headlights at night and occasionally on the wrong side of the road. When one participant in a newspaper survey was asked 'When is it permissible to overtake on the inside?' (this is illegal in Argentina) his response was 'When you're in a hurry!' And don't think it's just the men who have no concept of the Highway Code. In Buenos Aires I've seen a woman driver fearlessly cut across six lanes of downtown traffic after spotting her best friend on the sidewalk.

Driving: the Argentine way

I experienced Argentine road etiquette firsthand when I caught a lift with Jesus and his nephew Angel (their real names, I swear) in the rugged northwest. Jesus had a large truck and was charitably taking any hitchhikers who were also heading to Salta, piled in the back with crates of peaches and hunks of goat's cheese. The trip was going swimmingly (we'd only had a handful of close shaves with oncoming vehicles and precipices) when a police roadblock loomed into view. As if on cue, all the drivers in the cars in front automatically reached for their seatbelts. But Jesus, who until then had struck me as the law-abiding type, swerved off the road like *Thelma and Louise*, and continued down a dirt track beside a canal, adding an extra hour to our journey.

'Why the detour?' I asked innocently.

'Oh,' said Jesus without hesitation. 'My license plate has fallen off, the brakes aren't working, my back light's shot through, I have passengers in the back without a permit and I haven't paid my tax for five years.'

WOMEN

Across Argentina, but particularly in Buenos Aires, women are groomed and coifed to perfection. Meticulous in her appearance, the Argentine woman always seeks to make the most of herself and avidly follows the latest fashions in Paris, Milan and New York. Her international reputation for beauty is well deserved. To be honest, most Argentine women wouldn't look out of place on the catwalk.

Understandably, she simply adores shopping, which she does frequently with her large number of female friends. She is also a huge fan of the hairdressers, dropping in at least once a week to be blow-dried and manicured (as do many Argentine men).

Clothes are very important; there is a popular saying that an Argentine woman dresses up for other women and undresses for men. As a woman, walking down the street you are just as likely to get eyeballed by other women checking out your clothes as by men checking out what's inside them.

An Argentine woman's most powerful weapon may well be her mascara wand, but this does not mean that she assumes the role of a second-class citizen. Back home it's clearly the women who rule the roost. (This can be seen in bars throughout the country when married men leap up and say, 'I've got to go home or my wife will kill me.') In their role as mother, Argentine women have attained a powerful, almost saint-like status at the centre of the all-important family. And young and old alike most assuredly know how to twist their men around their little finger, exercising every female wile in the book that seems to come naturally from childhood.

They are also a smart, well-educated lot. University places are divided 50-50 between the sexes and women are already overtaking men in the medical profession. Unfortunately, however, while there are famous actresses and models, it is still rare for a woman to gain renown through business or politics. But on the stage and catwalk, they excel. Many Argentines grace the international catwalks and the covers of fashion magazines. Two of the greatest TV stars today in Argentina are women who host their own shows, command

Cosmopolitan Buenos Aires is a haven for Argentine women who love to shop.

millions a year and make the rules for when and with whom they will appear. So, in spite of all the machismo undercurrents at work, it's probably not such a man's world after all.

Eating Disorders

Just as low fat yogurt is an Argentine woman's best friend, bulge is her greatest enemy. I don't think I have ever once seen any of my female Argentine friends eat the complimentary biscuit that arrived with their espresso, let alone bite into a chocolate bar without feeling awash with guilt. To put it bluntly, being overweight in Argentina is socially unacceptable. Partly thanks to attitudes like this, Argentina is now in the unenviable position of topping the world charts for eating disorders. Experts are desperate to raise the alarm that the ever-increasing social pressure on Argentine women to be thin poses a serious threat to the nation's health.

There is such a huge and unfair pressure on women to be beautiful and, more importantly, thin in Argentina. Some blame this on a macho society were women are judged primarily on their looks. Others blame it on the general Argentine obsession with appearance.

'We live in a very materialist culture with superficial values,' psychologist Paula Morinigo said. 'One in every four advertisements mentions the body, everything is to do with diets and it's all very easy to get hold of.' Just walking around any town in Argentina, you'll be bombarded with advertisements promising the key to a perfect body. Supermarket shelves are stacked with diet products; laxatives and slimming pills are selling like hot cakes in pharmacies, and these days if you order a coke in one of Buenos Aires' famous cafés, chances are (if you're female) you'll be asked, 'Will that be Diet Coke?'

'In Argentina people just assume all girls are on a diet. Everyone is constantly talking about new diets and how much and what they eat,' says my

A Model Career

A recent survey revealed that the main ambition of two-thirds of Argentine schoolgirls is to become a model.

friend Anna, a 23-year-old university student, and herself a former bulimic. 'When you get on a bus in Buenos Aires all the other girls eye you up and down, it's like a competition as to who is the thinnest or most beautiful and here you can only be beautiful if you are thin.'

This pressure isn't just on adolescents and young women—the traditional victims of eating disorders—but is also increasingly being felt by men (12 per cent of patients treated in Buenos Aires' clinics for eating disorders are male), older women and small children.

'Even young children are worried about their appearance,' says Dr Mabel Bello of the *Asociacion de Lucha contra Bulimia y Anorexia*. 'If you ask a school kid what do you want to be when you grow up, they'll answer, "thin". Dr Bello has treated patients as young as 5 and 6 years old with severe bulimia and anorexia at her clinic in downtown Buenos Aires. 'In these cases there has usually been pressure from the family with a severe body culture. Some parents even put artificial sweetener in their baby's food.'

Such an alarming obsession with dieting couldn't have happened in a more unsuitable country. People love to go out and socialize in Argentina and practically every social occasion involves food, be it the Sunday barbecue or dinner with friends over an enormous bowl of pasta. So how on earth do you manage to resist Argentina's famously delicious food, I asked my skinny friends? 'Oh, we just smoke and drink *mate*,' came the response.

Plastic Surgeons and Personal Trainers

If they're not starving or smoking themselves thin, many Argentine women may put themselves through grueling exercise regimes in their quest to escape the dreaded spread. Television advertisements sell all sorts of hideous looking contraptions that promise to improve your physique. One —was it for a chastity belt?—bragged that it could make your bottom look 'nice and pert, just how men like it'.

In the ongoing quest to be body beautiful, many Argentines have resorted to the surgeon's knife, to nip and tuck, augment and reduce their various body parts, including, so they say, footballer Diego Maradona and former President Carlos Menem. The latter, at least, had the political sense to tell the nation that the giveaway bruising was from a nasty wasp sting.

Plastic surgery isn't the exclusive field of Argentina's rich and famous. Special summer deals, payment by interest-free installments and reduced rates if you have more than one operation mean that plastic surgery is available to just about anyone who really wants it that badly. Just when I thought I had become immune to all the jutting cheekbones, hip bones, alarmingly high hairlines and collagen-enhanced lips on the streets of Buenos Aires, I had my own mini culture shock when three lovely blonde sisters told me they'd all been given

Beautiful People

One in 30 Argentines is estimated to have gone under the plastic surgeon's knife making this the most operated on population in the world after the US and Mexico.

breast implants as 21st birthday presents from their mother.

If the surgeon's knife is too much to stomach, personal fitness trainers are now very much in vogue, especially among the *farándula*—Argentina's 'in' crowd of TV stars, models and playboys. You can hardly blame them. The *farándula* come under permanent scrutiny from the weekly gossip magazines whose headlines frequently read something along the lines of 'Moira/ Susana/Graciela is looking fabulous, having lost 10 kilos in a fortnight' or (*gasp!*) 'so-and-so has let herself go'—a heinous crime in Argentina.

The Mothers of the Plaza de Mayo

Just when you're starting to think you're in Beverly Hills rather than South America, you'll suddenly be brought down to earth with a shocking jolt. An article in a newspaper, something on television or even a passing flash of graffiti as your taxi races round a corner reminds you that Argentina has also lived through some dreadful dark days. If you're in Buenos Aires on a Thursday afternoon this reminder becomes even more poignant with the presence of a group of elderly women in the Plaza de Mayo.

At first sight, you might think these women are merely out for an afternoon stroll, but then you notice that they're all wearing white scarves on their heads, some are wearing badges, and they are holding placards with photos of young men or women. These photos are of their children and underneath is written the desperate plea, 'Where are they now?' Their children are the 'disappeared', some of the thousands of Argentines who were tortured and killed or just simply disappeared during the *Proceso*—a time when the military government declared an all-out 'Dirty War' against people they considered subversives.

These are Argentina's best-known mothers, gutsy, tough and fearless women who have taken on successive military and democratic governments in their search for truth and justice. They are known as 'the Mothers of the Plaza de Mayo' and have performed this weekly ritual since 1977, when a group of women first converged on the Plaza de Mayo to demand the whereabouts of their disappeared children and call for their murderers to be brought to justice. Their pain must be immeasurable, yet the mothers have never faltered in their demands and the search for their children and loved ones, even when faced with government threats and intimidation. As you can well imagine, the mothers are held in high regard in Argentina and their unceasing protests have come to represent the national conscience for the atrocities of the Dirty War.

I met one of the mothers, Margarita Peralta Gropper, in their office in Buenos Aires. 'I'm not in the house very often on my own, but when I am that's when I start to think about my poor boy and of the torture. It makes me sick,' said Margarita, whose son disappeared in 1977 when he was abducted from their house in Buenos Aires and taken away, she believes, to a clandestine torture centre.

'I couldn't do anything there, they took my son away and I couldn't get him back or ask for him, nothing. If he'd been

The mothers of Plaza de Mayo resiliently keep to their mission of seeking their lost loved ones through their weekly ritual.

in a police station or somewhere we knew I could have done something, but there, with the army, I was helpless and so was my son.'

Like so many innocent victims killed during the Dirty War, Margarita says her son was not even politically active. 'To this day I still don't know why they took him away. Sure he knew about politics as much as the rest of us but he didn't have any political affiliations, he just wanted to help everybody. He was everybody's friend, the best *compañero*.'

For Margarita, as for thousands of other mothers, it soon became clear that her son was never going to reappear alive. 'After an investigation told us that all the disappeared were presumed dead, my husband went white and grabbed his chest. Five days later he was dead,' said Margarita. 'Many other parents committed suicide or died. They didn't die of illness, they died of desperation.'

PSYCHOANALYSTS

Argentines, *porteños* in particular, tend to spend a disproportionate amount of their spare time—and money—probing their psyches on the analyst's couch. Maybe such an addiction to therapy is an understandable offshoot of having lived through such atrocious times, of disappearances, torture, military governments and economic meltdown. But psychoanalysis has actually been popular in Argentina since the 1960s.

Curious, it wasn't long before I started to make inquiries and was astonished to discover that nearly everybody I knew in Buenos Aires was in therapy for various and mysterious reasons. Even the psychoanalysts I met saw psychoanalysts, and trade unions and industrial organizations frequently look upon psychotherapy as an essential part of employees' benefit package.

One of my flatmates fell in love with his psychoanalyst and the subsequent break-up with her was so traumatic that he booked six months of sessions with another psychoanalyst. My flatmate, like most of my other friends in therapy, was permanently strapped for cash.

In Buenos Aires there are reputedly more psychoanalysts per capita than anywhere else in the world, and three times more than in New York state.

Yet it appeared that he'd literally rather go without food than skip a session. 'If you're sick, you don't think twice about paying to see a doctor,' he told me. 'So why shouldn't we go and see our psychoanalysts when we've got problems?'

No one is in any way ashamed or tries to hide the fact that they are in therapy. On the contrary, a weekly visit to your psychoanalyst is considered the most natural thing in the world—rather like going to the hairdresser. You can't help feeling that having a psychoanalyst is something of a status symbol, rather like having a personal trainer.

As a result of this national obsession, conversations with your Argentine friends may be peppered with psychobabble: *trauma*, *oral fixation*, *according to my psychoanalyst* frequently pop up. Friends may discuss the merits of various treatments and swap names and addresses of their psychoanalysts. If you don't want to feel left out, try getting to grips with the works of Freud and Jacques Lacan, the main texts used among Argentina's psychoanalysts. Better still, if you really want to throw yourself into the culture, get your own psychoanalyst. You'll be spoilt for choice.

In the fierce competition, many psychoanalysts have sought to specialize. One newspaper carried an advertisement for a Christian psychoanalyst whose bold claim was that he'd read the bible. Another advertisement aimed to corner the gringo market by offering counseling for foreigners 'having problems adapting to life in Argentina'. Whether all this psychoanalysis is a 'chicken or egg' thing or a profound problem with the Argentine psyche, nobody's too sure. But psychology students at least—and there are many in Argentina—know that they're on to a good thing.

'Why are so many Argentines addicted to psychoanalysis?' I asked Dr Jorge Garzareli, one of Buenos Aires' leading psychoanalysts. 'I think it's because of our origins. We come from all over the world and grew up very fast. We're still trying to get information about our roles in society and find our place in the world.'

MRS JONES' CREAM TEAS

Argentina's immigrant legacy never fails to turn up fascinating histories and anecdotes, yet it is undoubtedly at its most bizarre in the Patagonian province of Chubut where, in 1865, the good ship *Mimosa* docked at Puerto Madryn and deposited 160 Welsh men and women on the shores of southern Argentina. In their quest to get away from the English, these enterprising Welsh had wound up in the isolated wastes of Patagonia, at that time utterly barren and still inhabited by bands of Tehuelche Indians. (Even today, Chubut is probably further enough away from anywhere to have escaped the lure of psychoanalysis and plastic surgery.) As they moved westward in search of arable farming land, the colonizers settled in villages and towns that they christened with Welsh names such as Gaimán, Rawson, Dolavon and Trelew. They were soon joined by 3,000 more Welsh immigrants; effectively creating what the Welsh minister Michael D. Jones dubbed 'a little Wales beyond Wales'.

Today, about 20,000 descendants of these early colonizers live in Argentina. Among them is Mrs Mirna Jones who serves up sumptuous cream teas to visiting tourists in her parlour at Ty Nain in Gaimán.

Mrs Jones' spread includes apple pie, lemon meringue, pumpkin jam, a decadent Black Forest gateaux and tea served

Mrs Jones reminicises about her Welsh ancestors in her tea parlour in Gaimán.

in the best china pots. The walls and tables of her tea parlour are covered with Welsh memorabilia and lace tablecloths, and a gramophone and an old church organ stand against a wall. Outside, rose bushes brave the Patagonian wind, clinging to the stonewalled cottage with sash windows that looks as if it has been directly transplanted from the real Welsh countryside.

'We don't just sell tea,' Mrs Jones told me in between bites of scones smothered in her delicious home-made jam, 'we sell tradition.' I think she was having a subtle dig at some of the new teahouses that have sprung up in the area, cashing in on the exotic appeal of tucking into Welsh cream teas in Patagonia. Mrs Jones, however, is the genuine article. She looks Welsh and, even though she has never actually been to Wales, knows how to speak Welsh. 'If we spoke Spanish to my grandparents they refused to answer us,' she remembers. But when it comes down to it, Mirna Jones has no doubts whatsoever as to her identity. 'We are Argentines. Our roots may be from somewhere else, but we definitely feel 100 per cent Argentine.'

OTHER LATIN AMERICANS

There's no doubt that Argentina is a country of immigrants from the Joneses of Patagonia to the Russian Jewish community of Buenos Aires. Yet a more recent wave of newcomers continues to pour into Argentina from neighboring Latin American countries. These immigrants, mainly from Bolivia, Peru, Paraguay and Chile, have come seeking work and a better life. Many of them, however, end up doing backbreaking work for little pay and live in miserable conditions. Unofficial estimates claim that over a million of non-Argentine Latin Americans now live and work illegally in Argentina. With their indigenous and *mestizo* looks that so easily differentiate them from the majority of Argentines, they have become easy targets for racism and are often blamed for escalating violence and for taking work away from Argentines. The truth is that most of these immigrants work the black market and remain largely excluded from the system. Often, they are even admired for their hard work ethic and for doing the type of jobs—such as shoeshining, plumbing and digging drains—which many Argentines would rather not do.

Ironically, although many of these immigrants lack civil and political rights, sometimes working in slave-like conditions, when they are caught by the police or immigration authorities, they actually leap to the defense of their bosses. When 45 undocumented Bolivian women, working 15–18 hour shifts in a clothing factory, were discovered by the authorities, they all spoke up for their employer, despite the fact that they had been forced to sleep on mattresses on the workshop floor and forbidden to leave the building. In Argentina they could still earn more than they could back home in Bolivia.

Many of the new immigrant arrivals live in the *villas miserias*, or shantytowns on the fringes of Argentina's cities, alongside many poor Argentine migrants from the provinces attracted by the hope of finding work in service and manufacturing industries. Some say that Argentina is too rich and too white to be considered Third World. Well, a visit to a villa—with its drop latrines, precarious housing, unpaved streets and pervading atmosphere of violence and crime—would soon change their minds.

THE POLICE

Few of the country's policemen even dare to enter the *villas miserias*, not that they'd have much success in catching any of the villains that seek refuge inside. 'The secret of survival is that you don't know anything, that you haven't seen anything,' said one inhabitant of a villa in an interview. 'The sneaks pay with their life.'

Even outside the villas, the average policeman on the street tends to be widely mistrusted by the public and this perception isn't helped by the fact that they have gained a trigger-happy reputation and reports of police brutality are rife. Many Argentines don't even bother to report crimes, believing at best that nothing will get resolved or at worst that the police themselves might be involved. Still, it can't be much fun being a policeman in Argentina. Armed shootouts are an increasingly common occurrence and many policemen hold down two jobs, working as private guards on the side to supplement their meager salaries. Others get paid under the table to patrol a certain area or 'earn' extra money through bribes. Frequently, a neighbourhood may club together to hire a private security guard—as clear a sign as any of a lack of faith in effectual policing.

FITTING INTO SOCIETY

CHAPTER 4

'Reveller!
Damn it, you're such fun.
Reveller!
A wasted man you are.'
—From the tango *Garufa* (1928),
lyrics by Roberto Fontaina and Victor Solino

SOCIAL CUSTOMS

The problem with adapting to life in Argentina is that sometimes it looks so familiar, you start to act as you would back home. So you go out to eat supper at a respectable 8:00 pm, but none of the restaurants have even opened yet. You've been stood up for an important engagement because there's been an unexpected snowfall and everybody you want to do business with is off skiing in Bariloche. People light up cigarettes in the supermarket queue in front of you without the slightest compunction and you just don't understand why you can't get a cup of coffee to take away.

The key here is to be open-minded, to expect the unusual and go along with it. Before you know it you'll find it impossible to believe that you ever drank decaf or went to bed before midnight.

GOING OUT

It's social suicide to be seen in a bar before midnight, and in a nightclub before two. Argentines go out as late as possible and stay out as late as possible. In fact, the later you arrive and the later you stay, the more fashionable you are. You'll soon discover that there's something delightfully decadent in partying till dawn, staying out for breakfast and frequently heading straight on to work. For weeks, I thought my Buenos Aires *barrio* was rather quiet until I realised that nine in the evening was far too early for the

local night owls—the place was absolutely heaving at three in the morning.

A word of warning. Don't think you can get away with the occasional late Friday or Saturday night, relying on Sunday to recover. Weekends, unofficially, start early here. The conventional weekend isn't enough for the Argentine party animal. Thursday night is generally considered the start of the weekend as regards going out until you drop, and this is frequently being pulled back now to Wednesday (even though both Thursday and Friday it is work as usual). If you do try and 'flake out' of going out you'll find little sympathy among your companions. You'll simply be told to *ponete las pilas*—put the batteries in—and join in the fun.

Fashionably Late

My first night on the tiles in Buenos Aires began around two in the morning. I'd given up any thoughts of going out when 12 o'clock chimed and my friend was still in her pyjamas nonchalantly eating ravioli. 'Bah,' I thought, 'these *porteños* are all talk and no do. They're not the party animals I'd been led to believe.' I couldn't have been more wrong. Like Cinderella's wilder sister, when two o'clock struck my friend leapt up, threw on a gold lamé dress and hailed a passing cab to take us to a multi-storey disco where we danced until seven in the morning.

And don't think that it's just the Capital Federal with the bright lights. Country folk they may be elsewhere, but when it comes to going out they're just as wild as their friends in the city, frequently worse. In fact, staying up all night is so common, Argentines tend to talk in terms of the 24-hour clock (otherwise a meeting at one o'clock might be a lunch date or a disco date) and they've even adopted a word to describe someone who stays up all night—*trasnochador*.

FLIRTING

One of the main reasons the Argentines love to go out so much is that it provides them with the perfect opportunity to indulge in their favourite national pastime: flirting. Argentines, both men and women, are fantastic flirts. Most everyday transactions, whether it's a quick visit to the local kiosk or buying the morning newspaper, will involve a certain amount of flirting. The butcher who hands your *bife* to you over the counter may do so with a wink or a raised eyebrow and the waitress who brings your coffee might catch your eye and hold it for just that little bit longer. The Argentine word for flirt, *coqueta*, however, can only apply to women. Argentine men will staunchly deny that they flirt, but they do.

Rodolfo, a flirtatious chef from La Plata, explained the situation to me: "Women flirt, men show off." He continued: "If I'm in a bar and I see a girl I like, it doesn't matter one bit if she doesn't show any interest in me, because that's when I begin to show off. First, I have to catch her eye and try to speak to her. She will, of course, ignore me (otherwise she is seen as easy). I will insist. If she carries on playing hard to get, I will begin to lie; I'll tell her about my Mercedes Benz, my great city job and so on. I will only give up if my advances are rejected five or six times and then I can't show my face in that bar again for weeks."

"The problem," adds Rodolfo after much thought, "is that women think that we men are only interested in sex."

The truth is, to a certain degree, Argentines are very much interested in sex. You only have to stroll throug' shopping mall or switch on the TV to realise that sex / in Argentina. Advertisements are saturated with bea and often scantily clad women, while those promoting products tend to employ impossibly glamorous girls dressed in minuscule skirts to hand out leaflets and free product samples. Nevertheless, flirting is always done in the best possible taste in Argentina, and it is largely an end in itself rather than a means to an end.

STREET LIFE

In the ongoing quest to see and be seen, Argentines take to the streets in large numbers. Weather permitting, as much as possible takes place outdoors. Cafés spill out onto the pavements under colourful umbrellas. Sash windows of restaurants are flung open to invite in the breeze and admiring glances. Bored and glamorous secretaries loll out of balconies five floors up above the traffic. And if there is a common gripe, my goodness, you'll soon know about it. Thousands will take to the streets in protest, clang their saucepans on the balconies, beat drums and let off bangers in some of the most exciting demonstrations you'll have seen in a long time.

With so much action going on outside, the streets become a key venue for campaigning politicians and businessmen. Cars with loudspeakers blare out music interspersed with announcements of new supermarkets or even lost pets. When things really hot up aeroplanes fly overhead and drop thousands of flyers onto the crowds down below. Street walls suddenly become ideal backdrops for murals and political propaganda. Political posters are layered on top of each other like wallpaper, and graffiti makes sure everyone knows exactly what everyone else thinks of the government.

But by far the most important outside event is *el paseo* (the stroll). In this respect, the Spanish plaza system, a relic from colonial times, provides the ideal location. You can happily circle the plaza in one direction while the object of your desire circles in the other. In Patagonia, no doubt due to the plunging temperatures, *el paseo* takes place in cars, which drive round and round the town centre. No one gets the slightest bit embarrassed to be seen driving round in circles eyeing each other up. The aim, you must remember, is to see and to be seen.

GREETING PEOPLE

Unless they're behind the wheel of a car, Argentines are some of the friendliest people on earth and greetings will generally be warm and effusive. Women kiss women, men kiss women, and men, if they know each other well, will also kiss other men. This is usually one kiss on the right cheek for both sexes. However, your first man-to-man meeting will probably begin with a hearty handshake.

The man-to-man kiss may come as a shock to many a male visitor to Argentina unaccustomed to bristly kisses. 'The first time my friend kissed me was awful,' said Alfredo, a Brazilian working in Buenos Aires. 'I was like, no no no, I'm not a homosexual. Then I realised that everybody did it.'

As a rule, if you enter a room you are to kiss everybody hello and as you leave you repeat the entire process and kiss everybody goodbye. If this is confusing, then lose your street cred and be the first to arrive. Then you'll be the receiver of all the kisses rather than the protagonist. The

Ever friendly and spontaneous, these Argentine teenage girls pose for a quick snapshot.

same rules apply if you bump into a friend on the street. You kiss him/her hello, then you must kiss everyone who is with your friend hello, and they in turn kiss all of your friends hello as well, even if none of them have ever met each other before.

In Argentina, you should never approach a stranger for information without first greeting that person with a *buenos días* (good morning), *buenas tardes* (good afternoon) or *buenas noches* (good evening). The same applies if you walk into a shop or a restaurant.

Finally, in the countryside and small villages it is customary to greet all those you pass on the road, even if you've never laid eyes on them before in your life. Obviously, for practical reasons at least, this is not done in cities or larger towns.

To Vos Or Not To Vos

Argentines can be quite informal and relaxed when addressing others. With people their own age or contemporaries they generally use the informal *vos* (the Argentine equivalent of the Spanish second person singular *tu*—meaning 'you') straight away, rather than the formal *usted* (you). Elders, business associates and people in important or bureaucratic positions, however, should be addressed as *usted*. If you are unsure of what to say, play it safe with *usted* until you are invited to use the informal expression. Informal they may be, but in the appropriate setting Argentines can be extremely title-conscious. University graduates may be addressed as *Licenciado*. Engineers are addressed as *Ingeniero* and architects are *Arquitecto*. Lawyers and doctors and PhDs are all addressed as *Doctor*. But people who are quite clearly neither PhD grads nor medical doctors may also be called *Doctor*. This is meant out of respect so don't make life difficult by asking exactly what they are a doctor of.

Che, Don't Call Me That!

Argentines are great fans of hoisting nicknames onto everyone they meet. Even as a foreigner, you will be no exception. This has the immediate effect of making life a lot more personal, which is how people like it. There is, however, one universal nickname which locals and visitors to Argentina will be called all the time—*Che*. It's practically impossible to give a literal translation of *Che*, it's something like 'buddy' or 'friend' or just 'hey you'. Even its origins are murky, but it is generally believed to be a derivation of the Mapuche Indian word for 'people'.

Your waiter can be called *Che*, so can your best friend, your taxi driver or just someone walking by of whom you want to ask the time. *Che* knows no class or sex boundaries. You just are. Thanks to the wide use of this word in Argentina, the Argentines as a race are often simply referred to as *Los Ches*. This is in fact how the Argentine-Cuban revolutionary Ernesto 'Che' Guevara got his nickname.

There are, however, many variations on the Che theme. You may be called *amigo* (friend) or *hermano* (brother). If you look Chinese, you could be called *chino*; if dark-skinned or black, you may be called *negro*. I know of one man who had large bushy eyebrows and was known as *cejudo*—the eyebrowed one—by his friends. For years Diego Maradona with his trademark flowing locks was known as *El Pelusa*, the straggly-haired one. If you're bald or have very short hair you might be known as *pelado* (baldy). If you're on the larger side you might get called *chancho* (piggy) or *gordo* (fatty). And if you're thin you'll be called *flaco* (skinny). Old people may be referred to as *viejo*, although probably not directly to their faces unless they are your parents—who will take it as a sign of affection. Most letters home in Argentina open with '*Queridos Viejos*', which is the equivalent of writing to your parents and opening with the rather curious greeting, 'My Dear Oldies'.

All this may seem shockingly racist, 'sizeist', 'ageist' and 'looksist' but no insult is meant at all, and strange as it may seem, it's actually meant affectionately. If you react with outrage to your new nickname, you'll simply be greeted with half-amused curiosity.

You should also take your nickname with a large pinch of salt. *Gordo* (fatty), for example, is frequently used as a term of endearment between husbands and wives, even if the are *flaco*. If the nickname is rounded off with an—*ito* on r end, then it's meant even more endearingly. *Gordo* becomes *gordito* (little fat one), *flaco—flaquito* (little skinny one) and so on. Even your real name can take on this diminutive: if your name is Carlos, you could be known as *Carlitos*.

Understandably, this degree of name-calling can play havoc with your self-image. "If someone calls me *gordita*, however endearingly, I hate them and swear to go on a diet," confided an Australian friend who was thin even by *porteño* standards. "But if they call me *flaca*, I'm on an immediate high and happily gorge myself on ice cream."

(Note: For women, the 'o' at the end is substituted with an 'a', thus *amigo* becomes *amiga*, *flaquito* becomes *flaquita* and so on. *Che*, however, is always *Che*, whatever your sex.)

MARRIAGE AND LOVE AFFAIRS

Like most social functions in Argentina, weddings start late and end late. Wedding jitters must be extra-exacerbated because the church ceremony usually takes place as late as 8:00 or 9:00 pm. This means that the wedding feast doesn't start until 10 to 11-ish and in some cases as late as midnight. The party proper, with live bands and dance floor, kicks off in the small hours. How they have any energy left for the honeymoon is anyone's guess

Children tend to live with their *viejos* until they get married, then they live with their spouses and new family.

High Divorce Rates

Divorce has been legal in Argentina since 1987 and Argentina holds claim to the dubious distinction of having South America's highest divorce rate. Divorcees, however, can't get remarried in a Catholic church.

Bachelor pads exist but they are an exception rather than the rule. As is 'living in sin', which remains something of a social taboo. This does not mean that all Argentines remain chaste until their wedding night. *Albergue transitorios* (hotels that rent rooms out by the hour) provide for young lovers, for those having affairs (Argentina is said to have the highest infidelity rate in the whole of South America) and even for happily married couples looking for a little privacy.

A couple sharing an intimate moment while enjoying the scenic view of the River de la Plata riverbank at Puerto Madero.

THE FAMILY

As in most Latin countries, the family is the central pillar of Argentine life. As a result families tend to be large and extended and relations generally live nearby. Argentine children will probably grow up with cousins as some of their best friends. Children are especially adored in Argentina and few screaming kids are told to shut up—instead they are lovingly humoured and welcome absolutely everywhere at anytime. It's easy to see how Argentines get into the habit of staying up late at an early age.

Growing Up

Like their mothers, Argentina's youth are sleek, glossy and generally impeccably dressed. There's no awkward adolescence for these kids; instead they seem to ooze confidence from a young age and are remarkably relaxed and chatty. One of the greatest social delights in Argentina is the complete ease with which the young and old interact with each other.

Two key events mark children's lives as they grow up. For girls, it is their 15th birthday or *quinceañera*, an

Bedecked in pretty dresses, three teenage girls indulge in happy chatter during their *quinceañera*.

important landmark to celebrate the end of girlhood and the transformation into a young woman. Given half a chance, the *quinceañera* can rapidly turn into a huge social affair involving expensive dresses, photos and maybe a slot in a magazine's society gossip pages. Occasionally, the whole family will take a celebratory trip to Miami or Disneyland, but more often than not parents will throw a big party at home for their daughter, where she dresses up in white and is given a large cake.

The other great excitement for Argentine teens is the riotous graduate trip (*viaje de egresados*). In this well-earned celebration for finishing high school, a large group of school friends, or even the whole class, go on holiday together for about ten days.

Practically every *viaje de egresados* takes place in Bariloche, thanks to this city's proliferation of discos and perpetual holiday atmosphere. Most graduate trips take place in November, when school breaks up, but many students go in the July vacation before they've officially graduated, for the skiing. For many, this is the first time they've ever been skiing, so they throw themselves into it with reckless abandon. If you don't like crowds and you're not 18 years old, it's probably a good idea to avoid Bariloche at these times of the year.

Tips on Socializing and Etiquette
- Always turn up a little late to any social invitations and never, ever arrive early.
- Remember to kiss everyone hello and goodbye
- If you want to stand any chance of keeping up all night with the *porteños*, squeeze in an afternoon/after-work nap.
- If in doubt about what to wear, overdress rather than underdress. Argentines always look fabulous.
- Remember that it's perfectly normal for complete strangers to bestow oohs and ahhs on babies and young children, ruffle their hair and pinch their cheeks.

ALTERNATIVE LIFESTYLES

Argentina is one of the most progressive countries in Latin America when it comes to gay rights and liberties. In 2003, Buenos Aires became the first Latin American city to legalize civil unions between same sex couples providing legal rights similar to those for heterosexual couples (excluding adoption and inheritance rights). Although this move was widely condemned by the Catholic Church, there remains among most Argentines a fairly relaxed 'live and let live' attitude. Certainly in the country's larger cities, there is an active gay scene with bars, nightclubs, magazines, gay-friendly hotels and even gay tango clubs. Sure, you probably won't see many male couples strolling down the street hand in hand, and socializing is on a fairly low-key level but Buenos Aires is rapidly gaining a reputation as one of the most gay-friendly places in Latin America. Thanks to this relaxed attitude, and fuelled by an favourable exchange rate, Buenos Aires is also increasingly becoming a key destination for gay tourism.

RELIGION

On the whole, Argentines take a fairly laid-back approach to religion. Real Sunday worship, they joke, takes place on the football pitch, even if the hordes of fans yelling and jumping around in the stands are anything but saintly. Church congregations are considerably smaller than you'd imagine in a country where 90 per cent of the population is Roman Catholic. In fact, less than 20 per cent of Argentina's Catholics are actively practising. A running joke claims that the rest of the country only goes to church for weddings and funerals.

But although the church pews aren't as packed as they could be on Sundays, few Argentines would ever dream of calling themselves atheists. On the contrary, religious beliefs run deep and form a very integral part of many Argentines' lives. Try and visit Luján, where a statue of the beloved patron saint of Argentina—the Virgin of Luján—is on display in the imposing twin-spired Gothic basilica. Sooner or later, most Argentines will make the trip to Luján that sees more than four million pilgrims a year. Many of Argentina's Catholics will also make the sign of the cross when they pass churches, cathedrals or religious altars. This can be especially nerve-wracking if you pass a church at high speed in a car, as it involves drivers removing their hands from the steering wheel in order to cross themselves.

> A popular Argentine joke: A priest and a taxi driver arrive at the gates of heaven but St Peter lets only the taxi driver enter. The priest asks St Peter, "Why didn't you let me go in too?" St Peter replies, "When you said mass nobody prayed, but when that taxi driver drove – everybody prayed."

Cars, buses and trucks are especially laden down with religious symbols. Hanging plastic rosaries weigh down rear-view mirrors and glittery stickers of the Madonna are glued onto windscreens (more often than not alongside pictures of scantily clad girls). A newspaper poll once revealed that most Argentines believe car crashes to be 'unavoidable acts of God'.

Although Catholicism is the official state religion, freedom of worship is written into the constitution. In addition to the Catholic majority, there are small religious groups, of which the main groups, Protestants and Jews, form 2 per cent of the population each. There is also an ever-growing Evangelical movement. (The city of Ushuaia in Tierra del Fuego, to take an exceptional example, has 12 Evangelical churches and only one Catholic church.)

Homegrown Religion

At first sight, Argentines appear to be fairly straightforward Catholics. But delve a little deeper, and it won't be long before you start raising your eyebrows. An example might be the hand-painted sign above the holy water in Salta's cathedral warning visitors, 'Don't throw it on the floor, don't use it as a remedy and don't use it for acts of witchcraft.'

As with the rest of Latin America, the Catholic faith that was brought over with the Spaniards over time incorporated many indigenous traditions. Although far from the scale of what happened in, for example, Bolivia or Mexico, Argentina has its share of unconventional rituals and ceremonies, especially in the country's northwestern provinces. In the Humahuaca valley, religious festivals may include ceremonies for the more pagan Andean earth mother (Pachamama).

An elaborate shrine dedicated to La Difunta Corrrea, located in Vallecito.

The Legend of La Difunta Correa

One of Argentina's strangest religious offshoots is the cult of La Difunta Correa. La Difunta—literally the decease—is the name given to Deolinda Correa who set out on foot with her infant son to follow her husband's battalion during the civil war in the 1840s. She eventually succumbed to hunger and thirst in the desert of San Juan. Yet when a group of soldiers stumbled upon her dead body some days later, to their amazement they discovered her baby son still nursing at her breast—alive and well. A miracle was declared and La Difunta Correa became an overnight sensation. It wasn't long before a shrine emerged just outside the small desert hamlet of Vallecito where her remains are buried. Thousands of Argentines make the pilgrimage to Vallecito each year where they leave La Difunta gifts and plastic bottles of water in thanks for miracles granted in her name. Literally hundreds of roadside shrines to La Difunta have been erected alongside the country's highways from Iguazú to southern Patagonia where long-distance truck drivers leave her the usual plastic bottles of water beside what look suspiciously like vital parts of their engines.

In Vallecito, dazzling shrines have sprung up around her grave filled with gifts that could stock a large department store. These are no ordinary trinkets but often incredibly precious and personal stuff. Among some of La Difunta's thank you presents are ponchos from Ecuador, a Black Virgin from Zaire and a troop of stuffed penguins from Patagonia. There are also electric guitars, university degrees, bandoneons, a double bass, hockey sticks, tennis rackets, swords, wedding rings and dresses, china plates, chainsaws and a moth-eaten stuffed Pekinese.

"What's on display is only a fraction of what we have," Gladys Heredia, administrator of the Vallecito site, told me before flinging open the doors of an enormous hangar stacked with hundreds of bicycles, cars, motorbikes and trucks left by more admirers.

La Difunta's supernatural powers and her enormous following are proving to be a headache for Argentina's Catholic hierarchy who, in spite of regular petitions, have refused point-blank to recognise La Difunta as an object of veneration.

"We tried to get the Pope to make her a saint," said a slightly miffed Gladys. "But he won't."

The Grateful Dead

La Difunta Correa's shrine in the San Juan desert is one of many graves across the country that attracts Argentines in their swarms. In fact veneration of the dead is so widespread in Argentina that the Argentines were once described as 'cadaver cultists'.

With a trip to the local cemetery seen as a perfectly normal thing to do on an afternoon out, you may feel that you've

stumbled across something out of the Addams Family. But death is big business in Argentina. There's nothing like the death of a famous Argentine to unite the country. When tango star and budding actor Carlos Gardel was cut down in his prime after the plane he was travelling in crashed in Colombia, the nation was beside itself with grief. And after Evita Perón died of cancer in 1952, huge numbers of the nation sank into uncontrollable grief—some distraught mourners had to be physically restrained from poisoning themselves at the foot of her glass coffin on display in the labour ministry. National heroes such as the great liberator General José de San Martín are remembered by the day of their death rather than their birth or for dates of historic greatness. And pilgrimages to the graves of the dead, both relatives and the famous, are a popular national pastime.

Even if cemeteries give you the creeps, you shouldn't miss out on a chance to join in this national fixation and take a peek into one of Argentina's famous necropolises. Not only do they provide fascinatingly morbid viewing, they are also a surprising source of insight into Argentine society itself.

The Cemetery Caretakers

During the day, Argentina's top cemeteries swarm with an army of caretakers who are paid by relatives to clean and maintain the family tomb. In Recoleta cemetery almost 100 people do the job. Among them is Francisco, who proved a most enlightened if not peculiar tour guide.

"Ghosts, pah! This is the most peaceful place on earth. Let's drink *mate*," he declared heartily and led me into a nearby tomb where his *mate* kettle was boiling on a camping stove. Perched on a coffin lid we drank our *mate* while Francisco, who like most Argentines boomed rather than spoke, divulged the secrets of Recoleta with cheerful glee.

The larger cemeteries are cities in themselves, with paved streets, tree-lined avenues and family tombs in every conceivable architectural style from Neoclassical to Art Nouveau, Gothic to Romantic. Inside these 'cities of the dead', tombs and mausoleums are crammed shoulder to shoulder along a maze of streets and passages. Chacarita cemetery in Buenos Aires, considered the largest urban cemetery in the world, is so vast that mourners can drive up to the tomb doors on numbered streets with parking spaces or buy a cup of coffee from one of the cemetery's peddlers.

Particularly creepy are the older tombs that have fallen into decay, where some coffin lids lie at awkward angles revealing death in all its ghastly glory. These mausoleums will eventually be reclaimed and sold to new families. Popular cemeteries have seen something of a boom in real estate prices. In Recoleta cemetery in the heart of Buenos Aires, tomb space goes for as much as US$70,000 for a few square metres, making this effectively one of the most expensive plots of land in the world. The plaques on the tombs here read like an Argentine 'Who's Who' with a dazzling string of former presidents, generals, poets and socialites. Indeed, so sought after is a slot in Recoleta, a local adage has it that you haven't really made it in Argentina if your remains don't end up there.

ENGLISH PIRATES AND THE MALVINAS

In a country of immigrants that is in so many other ways disjointed, the Malvinas (or Falkland Islands) remain a symbol of national identity and their potential to stir up patriotic fervour is never far off: the fact that they were 'unfairly usurped by English pirates in 1833' is one of the few opinions that most Argentines will wholeheartedly agree. If you are keen to fit in to Argentine society it's never a bad idea to brush up on the history of these obscure windswept South Atlantic islands.

The Malvinas are probably better known to the rest of the English-speaking world as the Falkland Islands. Yet, in Argentina even the most committed Anglophiles would never dream of referring to them as anything other than Las Malvinas (just as Port Stanley, the capital, is known as nothing other than Puerto Argentino). Consisting of two main islands and about 200 small islets, which together add up to an area no larger than Wales, Las Malvinas lie some 480 kilometres off the shore of southern Patagonia in the South Atlantic Ocean. Treeless and barren, the mainstay of the economy for the 1,800 islanders—known by the Argentines as kelpers after the local seaweed—is sheep (all 650,000 of them).

The history of these small windswept bastions of the South Atlantic has a lot to answer for in the current international wrangle. Since their first undisputed sighting by a Dutchman in 1598, the islands have been claimed and colonized at one time or another by Britain, Spain, France and Argentina. But in 1833 British forces expelled the Argentine colony and brought the islands firmly under British rule. Since then, the islands have been officially ruled by the British but unrelentingly claimed by the Argentines. For the Argentines, this isn't so much a question of right or wrong. It's just a fundamental and unshakeable belief that the islands were, are and always will be theirs.

The first thing any visitor to Argentina will probably read will be the words Las Malvinas son Argentinas—'The Malvinas are Argentine'. This mantra is strategically placed on signposts at every port of entry. The sign catches the sunlight in the extreme north on the Bolivian border at nearly 4,000 metres above sea level. It is there at the steamy Iguazú Falls for anyone who might come across from Brazil. You may see it along the ridge of the Andes at the Chilean frontier and, just in case you arrived by plane, it appears on billboards above the motorway that brings you in from Ezeiza airport.

The South Atlantic War

On 2 April 1982, Argentine troops invaded the Malvinas/ Falkland Islands, easily ousted the token British force and claimed the islands as their own. The moment couldn't have been more opportune for General Galtieri, the increasingly unpopular head of the military junta ruling the country. When he declared that Argentina was reclaiming what was rightfully hers, the country's dire economic troubles and sinister 'disappearances' were momentarily forgotten.

But Galtieri underestimated the response of Margaret Thatcher's government and a massive British task force steamed full ahead for the South Atlantic. The ensuing war was to last 72 days, claim over a thousand lives and cost US$ 2 billion. Many of those killed were Argentines—more than 300 died when the Argentine cruiser *General Belgrano* was torpedoed and sunk outside the national exclusion zone. This particular incident causes much pain and anger even today. The Argentine forces wreaked their fair share of damage with their deadly Exocet missiles, sinking *HMS Sheffield* and other British ships but they were soon overwhelmed by the British forces and surrendered in Port Stanley on 14 June. Over 10,000 Argentines were captured; many of them badly trained and poorly equipped young (often teenage) conscripts.

All maps in Argentina show the Falkland Islands in the national colours of light blue. If the maps are imported, then Falkland Is. (GB) will have been scratched out and replaced with Las Malvinas (Arg). The claim is so intrinsic that the islands are religiously included in all country weather reports, every major city has at least one street named after them and 10 June—Malvinas Day—is a national holiday.

The military junta and the armed forces were thoroughly discredited by the defeat and Galtieri was booted out of office. Meanwhile, the islands' status became more entrenched, with the 1,800 English-speaking islanders digging in their heels even further and refusing point-blank to ever accept Argentine sovereignty.

SETTLING IN

CHAPTER 5

'Mad dogs and Englishmen go out in the midday sun. ...
Argentines sleep firmly from twelve to one ...'
—Noel Coward

ARGENTINA ISN'T THE SORT OF COUNTRY where things are going to run without a hitch. This, undoubtedly, is part of its appeal. In the worst case scenario, you're going to find yourself up against enormous quantities of *viveza criolla*, a bureaucratic minefield and some of the most terrifying driving on earth. But do remember that however bogged down or lost you get, in Argentina there will always be someone happy to help you out. The following should help those planning on setting up and settling down in Argentina.

VISAS

A valid passport is required for all those wishing to enter Argentina.

Entry visas are not required for tourists from Andorra, Australia, Austria, Barbados, Belgium, Bolivia, Brazil, Canada, Chile, Colombia, Costa Rica, Croatia, Denmark, Dominican Republic, Ecuador, El Salvador, Finland, France, Germany, Great Britain, Greece, Guatemala, Haiti, Honduras, Hong Kong, Hungary, Ireland, Israel, Italy, Jamaica, Japan, Liechtenstein, Luxembourg, Malaysia, Malta, Mexico, Monaco, the Netherlands, Nicaragua, Norway, New Zealand, Panama, Paraguay, Peru, Poland, Portugal, Slovenia, Spain, South Africa, Sweden, Switzerland, Turkey, Uruguay, the United States, Venezuela and Yugoslavia. But visitors from these countries must obtain a free tourist card valid for 90 days upon entering Argentina. Tourist cards may be unavailable at smaller border crossings. Don't worry if you never get a tourist card, or even lose your tourist card. In a country where bureaucracy is alive and kicking, immigration guards can still be surprisingly relaxed and you can fill one out on departure. The tourist card can be renewed for a further 90 days from the *Dirección Nacional de Migraciones* (see Resource Guide for further details) although the extension will set you back US$ 100 and a fair bit of time. In truth most tourists find it easier to pay a visit to neighbouring Uruguay or Chile for a day or two before returning to Argentina on another 90-day tourist card.

Visa Documents

The following documents will be required for those applying for a visa from their Argentine consulate:
- Valid passport
- Certified birth certificate
- Four standard-sized passport photographs
- Payment of the application fee

In addition you may also be obliged to produce the following documents:
- Medical examination report
- Bank reference as well as documentation that give proof of sufficient economic funds
- Confirmation of enrolment in an Argentine institution (for student visas)
- Letter of introduction from employer in Argentina (for work visas)
- Return ticket

A visa is required prior to departure for citizens of all the countries not mentioned above, and is available from the local Argentine consulate. The official line is that all visitors on business require a visa, but most business travellers who plan to spend no more than 90 days in the country enter on the tourist card, thus avoiding unnecessary red tape. If you think you're going to attract a lot of attention because of the nature of your business or plan to stay for more than 90 days, you should obtain a valid business visa before you leave.

Long-term residence permits are also available but you will need to contact your local Argentine consulate well in advance of your departure. This visa will enable you to get hold of an Argentine ID card, which you'll need to open bank accounts and pay taxes.

Those wishing to work in Argentina must obtain a work visa from the Argentine consulate in their home country before travelling to Argentina. The Argentine company that plans to employ you is required to apply for the visa on your behalf in Argentina. There is a charge of about US$ 330. Work visas—which last for between one and three years—can also be obtained within Argentina from the *Dirección Nacional de Migraciones* but it is a long-drawn-out bureaucratic process that can last several months, and you may even be required to leave the country until the visa is secured. Those wishing to study in Argentina are also obliged to obtain a study visa from their local Argentine consulate before travelling to Argentina. Study visas, which cost about US$ 200, are valid for one year and may be renewed.

Visitors to Argentina are allowed to bring in up to 2 litres of spirits, 100 cigarettes and 30 cigars tax-free. No duty is levied on clothing, personal effects or used electronic items, but you may encounter problems if you are bringing in duplicate articles.

Finally, if you were born in Argentina but hold current citizenship in another country don't leap onto that Aerolineas Argentinas flight without first clearing your status. Under Argentine law all those born in Argentina except children of visiting diplomats are considered Argentine citizens for life and thus subject to the military draft and other obligations. Obligatory military service, however, was abolished in 1994.

Children under the age of 18 years travelling without both parents need a notarized document certifying that both parents agree to their travel.

ACCOMMODATION

Accommodation in Argentina caters for every taste. There are sparkling new apartments fashioned after Miami for the modernists out there; then again you might be seduced by an enchanting tiled courtyard or an overgrown balcony in a turn-of-the-century building. If you choose an older building, brace yourself for a series of Heath Robinson-like contraptions held together with sticky tape, unravelled paper clips and a terrifying system of exposed wiring. (The loo in my apartment had to be flushed with an old telephone cable.) But whatever its state, the Argentine's house is his castle and great pride is taken in keeping it spotless and gleaming.

Budget travellers should visit http://www.hostels.org.ar, which lists international hostels. You should also be able to make reservations through the website. Local tourist offices can provide a list of *casas de familia* (inexpensive family-run bed-and-breakfasts), a good budget alternative and not as anonymous as larger hotels.

Hotels

These range from luxurious five-star hotels such as the grandiose Alvear Palace Hotel in Buenos Aires to raucous hostels filled with a young international crowd of backpackers squeezed into bunk beds and sharing a communal kitchen. For the latter, try and get hold of an International Youth Hostel Card or an International Student Identity Card before you arrive and be sure to flash it and ask for a discount as you check in. Argentines themselves love to travel, so whatever type of hotel you choose to stay in, you will almost certainly mingle just as much with Argentines as with other foreigners.

A youth hostel may be known as a *hostal* or an *albergue juvenil* in Argentina. Make sure you're understood. I once spent hours trawling the streets of Tucumán asking for an *albergue*, only to be answered by baffled red faces. A kindly gentleman finally informed me that as far as he was concerned an *albergue* was a place young lovers went for an hour or so. The full name of these love motels is *albergue transitorios*. They are also known as *telos* in the local slang—but you probably won't walk into one by accident as they have obvious names like 'You and Me', red lights and discreet parking.

Estancias

To find the real heart of Argentina's Interior, you shouldn't miss out on an opportunity to visit an *estancia*. *Estancia* is the Argentine word for 'ranch', but it can stretch to mean anything from a large country estate of thousands of acres to a small working farm. *Estancias* can be found throughout the Interior, from *yerba mate* plantations in the north to grain and cattle ranches of the pampas and vast sheep stations in Patagonia.

With changing times, many *estancias* are no longer financially self-supporting in the traditional way and, luckily for us, have opened their doors to paying houseguests to supplement their income. Here you can observe the life of a working *estancia*—not much changed since their heyday in the mid-19th century—and participate in country pursuits such as riding, polo, canoeing, bird watching or simply relaxing round the family swimming pool before tucking into a massive *asado*. *Estancias* are ideal weekend breaks for both *porteños* and expats who long to get away from the frenzied buzz of the city.

Houses and Apartments

Of course, if you're planning on staying in Argentina for a certain amount of time, you will doubtless consider renting or even buying an apartment. Like all transactions in Argentina, contacts will be crucial. Without them, renting can become a strategic nightmare. You will be required to procure a guarantor (a person who is a home-owner themselves and an Argentine resident who will be legally bound to pay your rent and bills should you fail to do so), one month's rent in advance, and one month's rent as deposit. Argentines themselves bank on family members to act as their guarantors, so it's seen as a good idea to stay on amicable terms with your parents before you move out. If you've come to Argentina for business, hopefully your company will volunteer to act as your guarantor.

For a cheaper and more straightforward option—generally without the need of a guarantor—look for a room in a shared house. These may be advertised in the classified section of newspapers and also by an easy-to-spot

High-rise apartment buildings, such as the one in the picture above, can be found throughout Buenos Aires.

sign saying *Habitación Disponible*, stuck on the wall of the house in question.

It's surprisingly difficult to find apartments where a young group of friends share an apartment, without the beady eye of an oldie looking over them. In Argentina, children and young people tend to live with their families until they are married. To move out prematurely still raises eyebrows and could imply that you have fallen out with your parents. I was lucky enough to find a room in a shared flat with seven other 20-somethings in Buenos Aires' downtrodden San Telmo neighbourhood. (None of them had fallen out with their parents.) It didn't matter that I had no stereo; the nightclub downstairs played great salsa from Wednesday through Saturday and if I switched off my bedroom light I got flashing disco lights to boot. Things got even better when upon further exploration I discovered I lived on the same street as a top tango bar, several all-night cafés and the president. With Argentina's rigid grid system, streets can run

Practically all property transactions in Argentina take place in hard cash (and always in US dollars)—you will literally have to hand over a suitcase of dollars to the seller.

for several kilometres and tend to keep the same name for their entire length.

The highlight of our building, however, was a fantastic gold and black cage-like elevator that must have been at least 100 years old and torpedoed its passengers up and down to the accompaniment of alarming noises. Although maximum capacity stated three people, as many as five of us would frequently pile in, and because of the complicated weight system we would plummet to the ground floor or groan upwards to the fifth. On particularly bad days we would even free-fall for several metres. I stopped using 'The Cage' altogether after reading a horrifying (unconfirmed) statistic that claimed someone crashes to their death in a broken elevator every two hours in Argentina.

Maybe it's the precarious elevator system that causes old houses and apartments to be religiously avoided by

Recycling

Just because that old filing cabinet or those worn-out curtains no longer appeal to you, it doesn't mean no one else will have them. What's old hat for you could be just what someone else is looking for. At night, many poorer folk and people from the *villas miserias* stroll through city streets looking for discarded items they can put to good use. So before you chuck something away, think again. Put it out on the pavement last thing at night and by morning, I guarantee, it will probably have found a new home. The same holds true for glass bottles and cardboard.

Argentines, who hanker after the new, modern apartments. Old buildings are rather seen as second-hand goods and, finances permitting, are gene-rally shunned. Understandably,

In some cities, but not Buenos Aires, foreigners may be required to have a special permit before they can buy real estate. Be warned, this can be an extremely long drawn-out process.

considering the idea of being lumbered with the bill when the crumbling walls, questionable plumbing and roof finally give way. Still, if you keep your eyes open, you could pick up a nice turn-of-the-century house for a fraction of the cost of a small modern apartment in a trendy neighbourhood.

Domestic Help

It's fairly common among middle-class families in Argentina to employ a maid. Maids can be hired on an hourly or, more commonly, monthly basis. They help with everything from laundry and cooking to childcare. Scan the classifieds of the English-language Buenos Aires Herald or look under *Personal Domestico* in the *Yellow Pages*.

Buying Property

If you decide to buy a house or apartment in Argentina (and, thanks to a favourable exchange rate, an increasing number of foreigners are doing exactly that), your first step will be to get yourself a CDI number (the Argentine equivalent of a social security number). You cannot buy a property without one. This relatively straightforward process will involve a trip to the local police station followed up with a visit to the tax office (just remember to always have several copies of your passport on hand). Your lawyer should also be able to apply for a CDI number on your behalf. Once you find a property that you want to purchase you will obviously have to make an offer. Most sellers are open to negotiation so it's a good idea to come in a little under the asking price. If your offer is accepted you will then be required to put down a cash deposit, usually about 30 per cent of the purchase price, and a date will then be set for the final title deed transfer into your name.

Argentine estate agents surprisingly charge the buyer a commission (usually about 3 per cent + VAT of the asking price) to purchase a property.

Guide to House Prices and Rentals

Prices and rents will always be highest in Buenos Aires, but you can count on the equivalent in the Interior at around 20 per cent less. Monthly rent is nearly always one per cent of the house price. In Argentina, properties are usually priced according to their size in square metres and modern properties will always sell (and rent) for considerably more than older properties. In Buenos Aires' swanky Puerto Madero district you could pay anything up to US$ 3,000 per sq meter. In Barrio Norte, another top notch BA barrio, you're looking at about US$ 1,100 to US$ 1,300 per square metre, while in fashionable Recoleta the going rate is between US$ 1,400 and US$ 1,900.

Pet Care

There seems to be a sort of adopt-a-stray policy in force in Argentina, and many locals have taken upon themselves the task of providing regular supplies of food and water to those cats and dogs that have fallen by the wayside.

Richer pets will be spoilt for choice, with a wealth of top-notch poodle parlours to pick from. And for those of you with dogs who just don't have the time to take them for walkies, there is no shortage of professional dog walkers, known as *pasaperros*, in Buenos Aires. The sight of these dog walkers, tangled in a web of leads with a dozen dogs at the other end of them, provides a wonderfully comical sight and has become a very *porteño* image. Oh, but do watch where you step on the sidewalk.

EDUCATION

At 96.2 per cent Argentina can boast one of Latin America's highest literacy rates, but faith in the public education system remains shaky. If they can afford it, Argentines will send their children to private schools rather than the state institutions. Part of the blame lies with lack of funds. Teachers' pay is

A husky pup gets a cuddle in Tierra del Fuego.

lousy and as a result many teachers work at two or three different schools to make ends meet. It's not unheard of for a teacher to simply not turn up for a class; chances are they're at their other job.

Education from preschool to university level is available free of charge in Argentina and is compulsory for all children up to 14 years of age. Primary school enrolment is close to 100 per cent of the school-age population, but drop out rates in secondary schools are relatively high. Secondary education lasts from five to seven years. The standard certificate is the *bachillerato*, which takes on average five years to complete. A technical or agricultural *bachillerato* takes six years to complete.

There are some 20 private universities in Argentina, although the country's 31 state universities are considered good on the whole, and for certain careers, such as medicine and architecture, better than private universities. State universities are free; a private university charges about US$ 350 a month, sometimes more. The standard of education will not necessarily be better in a private university, but facilities, organisation and administration are considered relatively superior—lessons, for example,

Dog-walking has never seemed so easy as this *passapero* dexterously handles her job without breaking a sweat!

generally start on time. Another advantage of the private system is that degree courses can be completed in five years while state universities require at least six years.

Most students continue living at home with their parents during college and so tend to go to universities in their home city. The general exception to this rule is the University of Córdoba. Argentina's oldest university takes an estimated six out of ten students from outside the area. Out-of-town students camp down in small pensións or boarding houses, sharing a single room with as many as five others.

Many students work to support themselves through university, especially by the time they reach their fourth, fifth or sixth year, even if they are still living at home with their parents.

As you might well imagine, Argentine students have a touch of the revolutionary about them—this is, after all, Che Guevara's homeland. (He studied medicine at Córdoba.) So don't be surprised to see Marxist book fairs, communist banners and cooperative-run cafés in the university grounds.

Parents who don't want to totally immerse their children in the Argentine education system can choose from several private primary and secondary schools in Argentina. Many of these are bilingual, and lessons are taught in English and Spanish (and other European languages) and may follow the British or American curriculum. Lessons in state schools are always in Spanish.

To enrol in a state school or university you will need either a residence or student visa, both obtainable from your local Argentine consulate.

HEALTH AND SAFETY

For years, Argentina could proudly boast of being one of the safest Latin American nations, provided you didn't get inside a car. In 2004, on average 20 people a day were killed on Argentina's roads. In 1997, 49 people were killed on public roads in Madrid, 62 in Paris and 73 in Rome. In the city of Buenos Aires 423 people were killed. I don't mean to scare you with gruesome statistics, but do be careful and keep your wits about you at all times—this applies to both pedestrians and drivers.

It is estimated that half of Argentina's annual road deaths could have been avoided had people been wearing their seatbelt at the time. Seatbelts are required by law, but generally people wear one only when they're within sight of a policeman. If you do decide to do the sensible thing and buckle up you will probably have to dig the seatbelts out from down the back of the car seats (if they're there at all) and brace yourself for sidelong glances that imply you're being cowardly and un-macho.

Unfortunately Argentina's roads are no longer the only danger for locals and visitors. Armed hold-ups and shoot-outs, although not a common occurrence, are not unheard of now, even in the smarter neighbourhoods. Gangs of armed thieves have been known to walk into restaurants and demand everyone's valuables. The economic crisis and an ever-widening gap between rich and poor have been singled out to blame. Always seek local advice on what and where is safe and what is considered unsafe.

Also be on your guard against bag snatchers and pickpockets, especially in crowded or touristy areas and in the big cities. The classic robbery is the 'mustard trick' —someone will squirt a bottle of sauce (usually mustard) over your clothes and an accomplice then offers to hold your bag while you clean yourself up. The accomplice will, of course, be long gone before you realize what's happened.

Don't even think about taking a handbag along to a football match. Football games can be dangerous and many fans are armed with knives and even guns. Argentina must be one of the few countries in the world where you face getting lynched for supporting the wrong team.

Health Hazards

The humidity in Buenos Aires (averaging 76 per cent) will make the winters seem colder and the summers hotter. Then there is the pollution to contend with. The newspaper *La Clarin* runs a daily chart of carbon monoxide pollution levels in Buenos Aires, which always seem to hover precariously close and frequently over the maximum tolerable line. It makes for interesting reading even though you can't do much about it. Asthma sufferers and those with sinus or bronchial problems may have trouble with heat and pollution in Buenos Aires and should also be aware that during the dry season unpaved roads can get very dusty indeed.

Always seek local advice before eating seafood, especially shellfish. The red tide (*marea roja*) periodically affects the coast of Argentina. It is deadly and warnings should not be taken lightly.

Creepy Crawlies and other Nasties

Argentines are sticklers for fumigation and men in white coats make regular house visits to spray into those dark corners. In Buenos Aires, they're usually after ants and cockroaches, which are quite a problem in the summer. South America's really nasty creepy crawlies don't make it as far south as Buenos Aires or Patagonia.

Further north, however, where it's hotter, and especially in low-lying tropical areas, it's advisable to take malaria pills. Obviously the best approach is to avoid being bitten by mosquitoes altogether. Dengue fever, which is prevalent in some areas, is also transmitted by mosquitoes. Other dangers in the north include leishmaniasis and Chagas' disease. Chagas' disease is transmitted through the bite of the vinchuca beetle, causing arteries to harden and long-term complications that eventually lead to death. The beetle likes *adobe* buildings with dirt floors and decrepit roofs and usually comes out at night, so avoid sleeping in such dwellings if you can. If you have no choice, tuck up your feet (the beetles go for these) and use a mosquito net. If you think you've been bitten by a vinchuca, seek medical advice immediately. If you've been in a malarial area and show symptoms even as late as a year after your trip, see a doctor immediately.

HIV/AIDS

HIV/Aids was first reported in Argentina in 1982 and in 2005 there were 130,000 known cases The majority of Aids victims are in the 20–34 age group and an increasingly higher number of women are being infected. Leading causes of infection are through intravenous drug use, sexual transmission and an HIV-positive mother. However, the HIV virus can also be contracted through medical and dental procedures involving the use of infected hypodermic or blood transfusion equipment. Where possible seek medical treatment only after consulting your embassy. Condoms, which can prevent the transmission of HIV and other sexually transmitted diseases, are widely available in Argentina despite this being a Catholic country.

Doctors and Medical Emergencies

In larger cities, you probably won't have too much trouble finding a doctor who speaks English (addresses of hospitals with English-speaking staff are listed in the Resource Guide). Many Argentines and most expats, if possible, sign up with a private health programme that covers medical and dental costs and includes an ambulance service. There are private and state hospitals (private ones undoubtedly provide better service). There is also a national ambulance emergency service (tel 107), but the running joke is that it's so slow you'll probably die of old age before it arrives.

MONEY, MONEY, MONEY

You should be able to change currency and withdraw savings from most Banks, Bureaux de Changes (*Casas de Cambio*) and Automated Teller Machines (ATMs). You can get away with handing over torn and dirty pesos, but dollars must to be in perfect condition. Cashing traveller's cheques can be quite difficult and the charges are often high. Many banks refuse to change certain types of traveller's cheques—if any at all. (American Express is widely considered the best.) ATMs throw out a confusing stream of Spanish, but often have an English translation and are unlikely to gobble your card. The green-and-yellow LINK sign or the red Banelco sign indicates machines that accept most of the major credit cards including Visa, MasterCard, Diners Club International and Cirrus.

You may also consider opening a local bank account. Provided you have all the correct documentation, including a residence visa and a valid passport, you would think that this should be fairly straightforward but unfortunately it can turn into something of a bureaucratic ordeal. For example, one foreign visitor's efforts to open an account were rejected because his passport number was 'too long'. His advice: 'Persist. It is possible.' Recommended banks include Bank Boston, HSBC Roberts, Banco Francés, Banco Galicia, Citibank and Banco Rio. Note that you may be charged a monthly fee for the privilege of having a current account or even a savings account.

One of the biggest money frustrations is that no one ever seems to have any change. At times a 100-peso note is as good as worthless. If a shopkeeper refuses to accept your note and demands that you come up with smaller change, stand your ground. They'll probably produce the change in the end. At smaller kiosks you may be encouraged to accept your change in the form of sweets or candy if the shopkeeper is out of small coins. Peso notes come in denominations of 100, 50, 20, 10, 5 and 2 pesos. There are coins for one peso and also for 50, 25, 10 and 5 centavos. No one ever has any 5-centavo coins so things are usually rounded off to the nearest 10 centavos.

Forgeries of both peso and dollar banknotes are common in Argentina, so take care when dealing with large amounts of cash.

The provinces of Jujuy, Salta and Tucumán use both pesos and a system known as *bonos*. *Bonos* look to all intents and purposes like useless scraps of paper and outside the province of issue they are no more than that (so make sure you leave the province without them). Within the province of issue, however, they are valid as currency.

Tipping and Bargaining

If a service charge is included on your restaurant bill, you are still expected to tip 5 per cent. If no service charge is included, add a tip of 10 per cent. In *parrillas* there is often a box where you can tip the *asador*. It is sweaty, hard work and, as you will undoubtedly be served such exquisite beef, any tip is well deserved.

Taxi drivers do not expect to get tips. In fact, the fare may well be rounded down rather than up. But if your *tachero* has been especially helpful, a tip will be appreciated.

Ushers in theatres expect a tip (about 10 per cent of the ticket price). And they should certainly be tipped should you take a programme or arrive late and have to be led to your seat in the dark.

Other people to tip include hairdressers; the man who loads your baggage into the hold in buses; porters in airports, bus stations, train stations and hotels; gas station attendants (if they fill the tank, clean the windshield or check the oil); and delivery servicemen.

Bargaining is not common in Argentina but you can ask for—and expect—a 10 per cent discount if paying cash in many shops.

Paying Bills

If possible, pay all your bills as soon as they arrive. Should you miss the payment deadline, you will enter a world of bureaucratic chaos. All bills must be paid in person at one of the places stated on the back of the bill. Put simply, the later you leave it to pay, the shorter your list of places where you can pay becomes. Ultimately, you will have to go directly to the gas board, electricity board or wherever and queue with hoards of others who had also left it to the last minute. There is a relatively new service called *Pago Facil* (Easy Pay) and you can now also pay your bills at places where this sign is shown.

TAXES

Buenos Aires itself originally flourished thanks to illegal smuggling and skilfully getting around Spain's colonial trade laws, and the legacy of tax evasion has survived to this day. Tax evasion, it is frequently joked, is a national sport in Argentina.

Needless to say, Argentina's tax authorities have long suspected that much is escaping them. They have tried to make collection procedures more efficient and close loopholes in the system, while simultaneously introducing heavy fines and even imprisonment for non-compliance. Still, they estimate that one-third of taxes due are not being paid. Tax dodgers argue that this high degree of tax evasion is justified by the high degree of government corruption.

As a foreigner conducting business in Argentina, don't even think about dodging your taxes. The bottom line is to comply with all the laws and regulations.

The finer ramifications of the Argentine tax system may be ambiguous and confusing, so it is a good idea to employ local specialists to guide you. At the time of writing, residents and resident corporations (those incorporated in Argentina) are taxed on worldwide income. Non-residents and non-resident corporations are taxed only on Argentine-source income. Corporate tax is payable at the rate of 35 per cent. Income tax rates for Argentine residents range progressively from 6 per cent to 35 per cent; for non-residents it is a flat rate of 35 per cent.

The federal government also imposes a capital gains tax, a value added tax (IVA in Spanish) on most goods at 21 per cent, a tax on assets, an excise tax and customs duties. Provincial governments are responsible for levying turnover tax, real estate tax, stamp tax, tax on vehicles and tax on public entertainment, among others.

Paying Taxes

If you work for an Argentine company, your employer is obliged to register you with the tax authority, file tax returns and retain taxes from your salary. If you are self-employed or earn an additional non-wage income, you must declare yourself at the tax office—*Dirección General Impositiva* (DGI). Tax returns for individuals are filed annually in June, when you declare your earnings for the previous calendar year.

Corporations are required to make 11 monthly advance payments, each at 8.5 per cent of the previous year's tax. The corporate tax return must be filed within five months after the end of the corporation's fiscal year.

ELECTRICITY

Electricity is supplied at 220 volts, 50 cycles AC. Plug fittings are either the European-style two round pins or the flat three-pin type. Adapters are available locally. Lamp fittings are the screw type.

MAIL

Outgoing airmail letters take about five days to reach the United States, seven days to reach Europe, and anything up to weeks in the other direction. Letters can be sent from post offices, larger hotels and mailboxes on the street—these are painted dark blue in the Interior and red in Buenos Aires. Incoming mail can be received at your home or office address; alternatively you can open a PO box at the *correo central* (post office) for three, six or 12 months at a time. The post office is open Monday to Friday from 8:00 am to 8:00 pm and on Saturday between 8:00 am and 1:00 pm.

Hopefully you'll be home when the postman arrives with a parcel. Otherwise, you must queue in the *correo central* where you will be given an eight-digit number. Even native Spanish speakers have trouble making out the numbers that are announced muffled through a loudspeaker. When your number's called, you pick up your parcel from a counter and bear in mind that it might be opened in front of you by a suspicious bureaucrat. "The whole experience was so humiliating," said an English friend, "that I asked my family to stop sending me things."

It is not completely unknown for post, in both directions, to go astray. If this worries you, send your mail from a post office; to be doubly safe, send it registered. Major international courier companies, including DHL, Federal Express and UPS, are represented in Argentina.

TELEPHONES

The cause of much fury and frustration, Argentina's telephone system is getting over its teething period and is finally on the road to recovery. Dialling a number is still often a matter of luck; you may reach your destination first time, but more frequently get a stranger growling that you're *equivocado* (wrong). Doubtless as a result partly of years of crossed lines and largely the expense of having a fixed line installed, Argentines have lapped up the mobile phone market. Argentina now has one of the highest number of mobile phones per capita in the world. The possession of the cell phone, rather like car ownership, is something of a status symbol. Argentines tend to wear them slung in holsters on their belts like urban cowboys; proud and ready to whip them out at the slightest high-pitched shrill.

It will probably be easier and cheaper to buy a mobile phone in Argentina (rather than bring one with you from home). But if you do find yourself phoneless, fear not: the country is well served by telephone centres (*locutorios*). There is at least one *locutorio* in each small town and hundreds in each city. The rates are far more competitive than making calls from hotels—which add significant surcharges—and the procedure couldn't be simpler: enter a numbered booth, make your call and settle up at the manned desk on your way out. Most of the larger *locutorios* also have Internet access.

A heavy rainstorm can still wipe out telephone lines, along with the electricity supply, for hours, even in Buenos Aires.

SHOPPING

Perhaps one of the reasons Argentines devote so much time to shopping is that it can be so much fun. Purchases, however insignificant, will be painstakingly wrapped in coloured tissue paper and ribbons and popped into bags along with the shop's calling card. Nearly all purchases can be delivered free of charge to your house and if you can't immediately foot the bill, a string of attractive options allows you to pay it off in interest-free instalments over many months.

They can look an intimidating bunch through the window, but shop assistants in Argentina couldn't be friendlier and more helpful. Window-shopping is tricky though, as you will be pounced upon as soon as you walk through the door and encouraged to purchase.

Clothes shopping for women can be traumatic. Those who take a 'medium' in the United States or Europe will find they are 'large' or even 'extra large' in Argentina. I have read one horror story of a girl who was entering a shop and was told to not even bother coming in as they had nothing in her size. Clothes are geared towards the Twiggy look where hipbones and ribcages are all the rage. Impossibly thin shop-window dummies have clothes pinned onto them to stop them falling off. This is especially the case in the flashy shopping malls where, if you're above a US size six, you can suffer a harrowing experience. Just as you're fleeing, near to tears because nothing fits, you'll be cornered by a stick insect thrusting a pamphlet from a 'slim centre' into your hand offering interest-free liposuction. But don't let shopping malls put you off. Larger-sized clothing is available away from chain stores and shopkeepers often add that personal touch.

As they do in other product and service areas, pharmacists, for example, will listen patiently to your symptoms, diagnose and prescribe, even (surprisingly) antibiotics. This may be a remarkably effective way of cutting out the middleman, but if it's serious medicine you're after, ideally you should go and see a doctor first.

Another personal favourite has to be the owners of ice cream parlours, who cleverly encourage you to taste spoonfuls of irresistible new flavours for free. There also seems to be a certain skill involved in balancing enormous amounts of ice cream into tiny cones. The result is a top heavy but deliciously generous serving; many visitors to Argentina claim the ice cream is the best they've ever eaten.

Shops open between 9am and 10am, and close around 6pm, 7pm or even 8pm in the evening. Shopping malls stay open even later. In the provinces, shops may well close between 1pm and 4pm for the siesta. Those that do will probably stay open late into the evening. Supermarkets may well remain open as late as 10:30 pm. In tune with the country's party atmosphere there's a chain of supermarkets called Disco. These are buzzing late at night when everyone seems to be out frantically last minute shopping for the typically late-night meal.

Incidentally, Argentina uses the metric system. Shoe and clothing sizes tend to be European although Argentines are increasingly using the English terms extra large, large, medium, small and of course extra small.

Kioskos

What would Argentina be without *el kiosko*? These wonderful local street stalls are the heart and soul of Argentina's cities, stocking just about anything you can think of—from hot dogs and cigarettes to chocolate and *yerba mate*—and often staying open long after the other shops have shut. After some time, your local kiosk vendor will become your best friend and if you don't have the right change, he'll probably just tell you to come back tomorrow. *Kioskos* vary in shape and size. They may be simple holes in the wall or quite elaborate affairs with plastic chairs and tables inside. The green tin newspaper kiosks are everybody's favourite, selling practically every newspaper, magazine, map and leaflet you can think of. And if they don't stock what you are looking for, then in true *kiosko* style, they will order it for you tomorrow.

Bookshops

Buenos Aires' bookshops, many of which stock second-hand books, are justifiably famous and open late into the night. You will be perfectly welcome to hang out for hours among the shelves and might even get away with reading an entire book without having to buy it. Buenos Aires also hosts South America's largest book fair in April, the *Fería Internacional del Libro*.

WHAT TO WEAR

If you plan to cavort with Argentina's rich and famous, you're going to need a wardrobe to rival James Bond's. Argentines—*porteños* in particular—are extremely fashion-conscious so come prepared to be eyed up and down. Men will find a suit and tie useful for formal occasions. Some nightclubs, casinos, restaurants and theatres have a dress code. A dinner jacket or an evening dress is also standard wear for a gala night at the opera or theatre. Should you take to the ski slopes, besides warm clothing you'll

One of the many bookshops in Buenos Aires that is open late into the night.

La Siesta

One of the greatest joys of life in Latin America is the siesta. This is a period that lasts several hours in the early afternoon, when everything is put on standby—shops close, businesses shut down and everybody goes home for a snooze or just to relax. The hotter the region, the more entrenched the siesta. And although the siesta has become a rarity in Buenos Aires and other big cities in Argentina, it is still a thoroughly important institution.

need something great to wear in the evening. Women who intend to dance the tango will find fishnet stockings and high heels indispensable.

Should you plan to see more than one season in Argentina your wardrobe will expand further. The fierce *sudestada* or southeasterly wind that blows up the Río de la Plata carries a considerable nip in the air as far north as Buenos Aires. In summer (November to March) temperatures can easily reach the high 30s (°C), and with Buenos Aires' high humidity it can be sweltering. So play it safe and come prepared for all meteorological eventualities. If you plan to go down to Patagonia or Tierra del Fuego, even in mid-summer (January and February) you'll need a large down jacket, woollen gloves, hat and, most importantly, something to keep the interminable wind out.

Don't forget to pack bikinis and shorts for beach outings. Beachwear is considerably more conservative than in Brazil and girls shouldn't even think about going topless. The one time a group of avant-garde beach babes tried to do this it created the most uproarious scandal and the TV cameras had a field day. Nightclubbing, however, can be as raunchy as you like. If in doubt, overdress rather than underdress and go for glamour every time.

TIMEKEEPING

Argentines are not big on punctuality, so try not to get too stressed if you are kept waiting. In fact, arriving at the appointed hour could be a social gaffe. For example, if you are invited to someone's home for dinner at 9:00 pm, don't even think of arriving before 9:30 pm, unless of course you plan to catch your hostess in the bath. Likewise, it's generally a good idea to be fashionably late for parties, drinks, nightclubs and other social events. There are exceptions:

you'll probably want to arrive on time for organised events such as a concert, even though these are not guaranteed to kick off on time. In a business setting, punctuality on your part is important even if your host rolls in late.

Every so often you get the distinct feeling that actually it's the 'done thing' to be seen as the last to arrive at a social gathering or even to board an aeroplane. Maybe, you think, they are really twirling their thumbs at home waiting for 3:00 am to roll on. But perhaps the most likely reason for this tardiness is that Argentines spend literally hours grooming and getting ready to go out. The end product is, without exception, always fabulous.

A punctilious English friend of mine, married to an Argentine, gets around this timekeeping problem by telling his wife that he wants to leave the house at least an hour before he actually intends to. That way his wife has plenty of time to get ready (and is what she believes to be fashionably late) and he gets to leave on time.

PLANES, TRAINS AND AUTOMOBILES

Driving in Argentina falls into a category somewhere between Mad Max and the Grand Prix. Drivers are happy to tackle any type of road, however dreadful, in whatever weather, but generally at some speed. In the cities, particularly in Buenos Aires, driving is exceptionally aggressive. If speed has to be cut because of rush hour congestion, the *porteño* driver will make up for lost time with vigorous lane hopping, honking, swerving out of the way of oncoming traffic at the last minute and taking corners on two wheels. Needless to say, there are frequent prangs accompanied by much shouting, exchanges of offensive hand signs and amazing strings of verbal abuse at other drivers. Often, after an accident, drivers get out onto the street to settle the argument as to who was the worse driver or whose fault it was, much to the amusement and delight of other motorists.

Buses

Bus drivers are widely respected and, of course, macho. In many rural areas buses are the only means of regular

Strangely enough, queues at bus stops are some of the most orderly in Argentina and are not usually barged

transport and the drivers may also act as postmen, paperboys and bread deliverers rolled in one. Argentina's major cities are connected by good bus links and the regional service is extensive, reaching smaller towns and villages. On long-distance buses (combis) there is usually air-conditioning and toilets on board. Prices are competitive, because many companies run the same routes.

City buses or *colectivos* are an institution in their own right, hurtling through the congested traffic at breakneck speed with passengers packed like sardines and clinging on for dear life around corners. Make sure you board with enough small change—banknotes won't do—to feed into the metallic machine that will spit out your ticket. Bus trips usually cost US$ 0.70 within the city centre and slightly more for trips to the suburbs. Hang on to your ticket for the duration of the journey in case of any spot checks.

You should always board the bus at the driver's end and alight at the rear. But be quick at both ends as the *colectivo* won't hang around. *Colectivo* drivers run on a tight schedule and can be understandably gruff, irritated by inspectors constantly breathing down their necks.

There are hundreds of different set bus routes in Buenos Aires and other large cities and the buses that run along them are all numbered. If you're lost, just ask any local, or better still, inquire at a nearby kiosk, about the best bus route to get where you want to go, and they'll point you to the appropriate *parada* (bus stop). It may also be worth getting your hands on a bus guide (see the Resource Guide).

Taxis

Unless you're a diehard adrenaline junkie, never ask your cabbie to step on it. Never ask them to slow down either—they might be offended. In Buenos Aires, with almost 40,000 cabs on the streets, it's easy to get a lift on any street at any time except when it's raining; *porteños* don't like getting wet. But with one cab for every 83 people in Buenos Aires —compared to, say, New York where there is one taxi for every 295, or London, with one for every 505—you're never going to have to wait too long. Taxis are black with a yellow roof and the flag-down fare is about US$ 1, rising steadily every 250 metres. Taxi rates are relatively good and cheap in Argentina—a ten-minute journey across downtown Buenos Aires should cost just US$ 4.

Once you know the sign, spotting a second-hand car for sale is easy. Argentines have invented an ingenious alternative to the straightforward 'For Sale' sign stuck on the windscreen. And although a sign may be put up, the more usual form is to stand an empty bottle on the roof of the proffered car (naturally, when parked). If the car interests you, simply inquire at the nearest household.

It is rare to find a taxi driver— or *tachero* as they are known in the local slang—lost for words. As in all countries throughout the world, but probably even more so in Argentina, your taxi driver will be a source of unbelievable amounts of local information. If anyone knows what's going on in town and why, it will be him (female taxi drivers are few and far between). Don't be afraid to strike up a conversation; they certainly won't.

For longer trips, such as to the airport, it may be best to employ the services of a *remise*. This is a private car with a driver that can be hired out for the day, a week or one long trip. For long journeys, they will generally be cheaper than taxis and prices are negotiable beforehand—but they don't drive any slower.

Most taxis are genuine but there are reports of occasional bogus drivers. Make sure the taxi you get into has a meter and a driver's ID hanging from the back seat. It is also recommended to flag down a moving taxi rather than one waiting on the curb.

Car Hire and Buying

If you are planning an extended stay, you may well consider hiring or even buying a vehicle. All the leading international car hire companies, including Hertz, Localiza and Budget, are represented in Argentina. The cheapest rates start at about US$ 30-US$ 60 a day. You must also be at least 21 and have a valid international driver's licence to supplement your local driver's licence. (Some agencies may require the hirer to be at least 25 years old and to have a credit card.)

You probably won't be able to pick up a good second-hand car for less than US$ 3,000 in Argentina. Popular models are Peugeot, Ford, Fiat and Renault. Do make sure you have the title to the car (known as a *tarjeta verde* or green card) and that your licence tax payments are up to date. It must also be fully insured (the more expensive the car, the more the insurance,). Foreigners will also need authorised permission to take a car bought in Argentina out of the country.

Driving Licence

If you already have a driving licence from your home country, before you leave get an international driver's licence, which, in conjunction with your original licence, is valid throughout Argentina. To be eligible for an Argentine driving licence, you must be at least 17 years old. You must pay a fee of US$ 100 at the municipal offices, and will be required to pass an eyesight test as well as a short and fairly easy driving test in an enclosed area. There are no compulsory lessons and no written exams. The licence is valid for five years, after which you must reapply.

Driving Tips

Numerous surveys have identified Argentina as having the highest number of road deaths. On average 8,000 people die each year on Argentina's roads—that's about one death every hour. Car accidents are the main cause of death among young Argentines and crashes periodically knock off Argentina's rich and famous.

It's not surprising then that all motorists are required by law to wear a seatbelt, carry a first-aid kit, a rigid tow bar, two warning triangles and a fire extinguisher. Few do. Transport laws in Argentina, like red lights, were made to be skipped.

If you do decide to take the plunge, drive on the right, brace yourself for a complicated system of one-way streets in cities and never back down in an argument with other motorists—it's simply not macho!

On national and provincial roads you will come across occasional police checkpoints, where drivers frantically reach to put on seatbelts, only to remove them again as soon as they are out of sight. If you are stopped by the transport police it is important that you can show your driver's licence,

Make sure you always travel with plenty of change as most roads have tollgates on them.

the green card (which proves your car is registered with the local council) and up-to-date insurance papers. If you fail to produce any of these on spec, you could face a heavy fine or, more commonly, be asked for a bribe.

Parking

Many cars have reinforced bumpers for the purpose of getting a large object into a very small parking space. On level ground it is unwise to leave your handbrake on. With this sort of parking going on, your car—if handbraked—will mount the neighbouring car, rather than just move along in a queue of pushed cars. Of course, it is inadvisable to park near a corner—you could get pushed out into the stream of traffic. In short, it is not unusual to find your car in a different place from where you left it.

Pedestrians

In Argentina, near-suicidal driving takes place on roads that are in a constant state of chaos and ongoing repair. Like the streets, pavements are riddled with holes ranging in size from small potholes to what could pass for mine shafts. Loose paving stones wobble and trip you up and shoot a jet of water up your leg as you step onto them. At the same time, the pedestrian is required to keep an eye out for water from air-conditioning outlets and dehumidifiers dripping from above. Surprisingly few locals come to grief. Argentines seem to have inbuilt radars for avoiding these obstacles while carrying on animated conversations, with frequent unexpected stops in mid-pavement to emphasise a point. Pedestrian traffic is much like road traffic—unpredictable and erratic.

As if all this wasn't bad enough, Buenos Aires also lays claim to arguably the 'world's widest road'. At its widest—some 20 lanes—the Avenida Nueve de Julio is every pedestrian's nightmare, but there's no avoiding it as it literally divides the Capital in two. Sooner or later any visitor to Buenos Aires has to take the plunge and cross it. The city council eventually took pity on the elderly and constructed concrete resting benches halfway across next to small blue signs that warn pedestrians to 'Avoid Accidents, Don't Run.' Who are they kidding? When the lights change to green and you're only halfway across with several tons of cold steel bearing down on you at top speed, believe me, run for your life.

A final word of warning: just when you think you're out of danger, a motorbike will whiz through a stream of stationary cars and mount the pavement. The rider may want to chat to a group of friends, deliver a pizza or just park, while giving you—the pedestrian—a mild coronary in the process. Motorbike helmets are simply a technicality; they are usually pushed up back off the forehead, adding an even more dashing dimension to these kamikaze riders. Bicycle helmets are unheard of.

Motor vehicles and pedestrians swarm the streets in a typical Buenos Aires traffic scene.

Don't get carried away by a sense of adventure and attempt to drive across this broken bridge in Patagonia!

Hitchhiking

Friends who have hitchhiked swear that it's the best way to get to know the country, provided you're patient and have plenty of time on your hands. Hitchhiking is relatively difficult in Argentina, but this hasn't stopped people from trying. Most trucking companies prohibit their drivers from giving lifts and even private car owners are wary since a highly publicised case of a hitchhiker suing the driver of the car he was travelling in after it crashed. Your best bet is to hang out at a gas station, or walk along the roadside and look hopeful. It's also a good idea to look clean and respectable.

Have a back-up plan (such as a tent and extra rations of food and water) in case you find yourself stuck in the middle of nowhere. Better still, try and make sure that you're always dropped off within walking distance of a town as you may get stranded for days—especially in Patagonia.

Remember that you are taking a risk when you hitchhike anywhere in the world.

Driving in Patagonia

Driving in Patagonia deserves a special mention purely because it couldn't be more different than anything you've done before. Argentine road veteran Dan Buck, who has regularly braved the Patagonian roads while doing research on Patagonia's famous outlaws Butch and Sundance, sums it up:

"Three animal species plague motorists in Patagonia: sheep, hares, and night drivers.

"Sheep are cute, fluffy, but maddening. Whatever direction a sheep is running, at the last second it'll run the opposite. Bounding along the roadside, angling away from your car, a sheep will pivot in front of you right when it's too late to hit the brakes. Whomp! Perversely, if the sheep is on a collision course with your left fender, just before impact it will execute an about-face. This is a guaranteed fact of nature.

"Hares, on the other hand, will do exactly what they'll look like they'll do. Leap out onto the road. Squish. Fortunately the *liebres*, as they are known locally, are multitudinous. They number in the tens of thousands, maybe millions (they won't sit down long enough to be counted). The dozens you flatten won't be missed.

"Night drivers, however, will unnerve even the most experienced on-the-road motorist. Night drivers in Patagonia use only one set of lights—high beams. There is nothing as harrowing as Ruta 40 on a moonless, coal-black night. Sheep zig and zag, hares dart through the air like so many furry locusts, and head-on round a dusty curve comes a pair of dazzling rockets of incandescent light that send you into a spasm of blindness, off the road, and into a ditch."

Aeroplanes

Argentina has several domestic airlines: Aerolineas Argentinas covers the entire country and the air force's passenger service Líneas Aéreas del Estado (LADE) specializes in flights to Patagonia. Domestic flights cost anything between US$ 125 to US$ 350 one way and some good deals can be found. Even though some airlines (Aerolineas Argentinas in particular) may charge foreigners more than nationals. Argentina's vast distances still make this the most viable option for traversing the country. With some flights, if you book in advance, you can get a much cheaper fare, so always ask if there are any promotions or discounts going.

Most international flights to and from Argentina arrive at Ezeiza Airport, 45-km (28-miles) from downtown Buenos Aires. Taxis and remises take you downtown for US$ 15 and a bus service run by Manuel Tienda León takes you there

or back for about US$ 7.50. There is an airport departure tax of US$ 18 for international flights. Domestic flights and those to Uruguay leave from downtown Buenos Aires at Jorge Newbery Airport; the departure tax is US$ 3 for domestic flights and US$ 8 for flights to Uruguay. Airport taxes are often included in the ticket price.

Trains

Argentina's once magnificent railway system has disintegrated over the years, receiving its final deathblow during the privatisation programme of the 1990s. Only a fraction of the main train services still run, and most of these go very slowly indeed, allowing passengers ample opportunity to admire the scenery.

Most of Argentina's railways were built by the British and were British-owned until they were nationalised under Perón in the 1940s. Many of the railway terminals, such as Retiro and Constitucion, hark back to Victorian Britain. The trains themselves are quite old-fashioned. There are also, however, more modern electric trains that connect downtown Buenos Aires with its suburbs.

Not only those wishing to travel will board the trains as they pull out of stations. A swarm of street vendors, selling

The Majestic Retiro station (above) was built to resemble British railway stations.

everything from biros to bibles, wade through the passengers depositing goods for sale on their laps, then wade back again collecting the money. If you don't want to buy the bible/biro/shaving kit/set of felt-tip pens, show no interest and they will eventually be removed from your lap.

For railway buffs, Argentina boasts its own great train journeys. One particularly arresting track known as the *Tren a las Nubes* (Train to the Clouds) is internationally renowned. Running from the city of Salta to the Chilean frontier, it is literally breathtaking when it reaches heights of over 4,000 metres and, at one stage, crosses *La Polvorilla*, an awesome iron viaduct. In true South American laid-back style, construction took almost 30 years, and by the time it opened in 1948 it wasn't of much use any more thanks to advances in air and road technology. Nowadays, the train runs mainly for tourists.

Other great train journeys include the 27-hour slog from Tucumán to Buenos Aires (if you want comfort, legroom and air-conditioning, travel Pullman class). The six-hour train journey from Buenos Aires to Mar del Plata provides

One of the entrances to the Pellegrini Subte Station.

a much safer option than the 400-km (248-mile) Route 2, alarmingly dubbed by local motorists 'the death route'. There is even a working railway in *Tierra de Fuego* (built by convicts) that can claim to be the southernmost train journey in the world.

El Subte

Buenos Aires' underground metro system, known as *el subte*, was built in 1913 with five main lines, four of which (A, B, D and E) run almost parallel to each other from downtown Buenos Aires to the northern and western suburbs. Only one line (Linea C) crosses them, connecting the major train stations of Constitucion and Retiro. Some *subte* carriages are wonderfully old and rattling affairs with wooden panels and gilded mirrors—although the doors don't necessarily always close before the train moves off. Many trains, however, have had their old carriages exchanged for more modern ones.

Providing they run in the direction you want to go, this is a fast and cheap option for traversing the city. Fares are just US$ 0.70 a trip (including changes, provided you stay underground). Buy up a bunch of tickets in advance, as this will save you having to queue at the ticket office every time you want to travel. You should also make sure you pass through the correct turnstile to the platform going in your direction or else you will have to leave and use another ticket to get back in.

Subte maps are available free of charge from *subte* ticket offices.

FOOD AND ENTERTAINING

'Their manners at table are ultra Bohemian. They read the papers, shout vehemently at each other, sprawl their limbs under and over the table, half swallow their knives, spit with true Yankee freedom on the carpeted floor, gesticulate and bend across the table in the heat of an argument, smoke cigarettes between the courses, and even while a course of which some of them do no partake is serving ...'
—19th century visitor Thomas Turner on Argentine table manners

EATING IN ARGENTINA IS NO MERE ROUTINE. It is an event, a fabulous social affair and the perfect excuse for what Argentines do best—socializing. Needless to say, Argentines are enormously arrogant about both their food and their cooking prowess. Beef, however, is the *pièce de résistance*. That their beef is the best in the world is a fact that will be stated to you frequently and quite categorically.

To crown it all, Argentines seem to have an inborn talent that enables them to cook their *bife* to perfection. Newly arrived in Argentina, I watched a *porteño* friend prepare a steak. With a lethally sharpened knife he sliced through the raw flesh like butter, casually dropped it into a frying pan, dexterously browned both sides with a skilful flip of his wrist and then set it down on the table in front of me—unashamedly bragging that it would be the best steak I would ever eat. Infuriatingly, it was.

WHAT'S ON THE MENU?

Argentina's menu reflects its migrant population. For a country that became rich on cattle, it's hardly surprising that beef dominates the menu. But the Italian influence can easily be seen in the abundant choice of pizza, pasta and delectable ice cream. Any standard restaurant menu will include an enormous variety of raviolis, cannellonis, spaghettis and lasagnas as well as steaks the size of small houses, all served with *papas fritas* (French fries) and crunchy salads.

(Argentines don't go in for green vegetables in a big way.)

Along with the Italians, other immigrants have introduced such delights as Welsh cream teas in Chubut, kosher meals in Buenos Aires and Alpine chocolate in Córdoba. In the northwest, where the Andean culture is still strong, spicy regional dishes are widely available. In short, you are unlikely to get bored or go hungry unless, of course, you're a strict vegetarian. Vegetarians get the short straw in Argentina. As a veggie, you'll be chastised and told that you're missing the best of Argentina. I've even known vegetarian friends who have been fed meat in disguise by baffled waiters who can't understand why on earth anyone wouldn't want to eat Argentine beef.

THE SACRED COW

In 1580, Juan de Garay drew up the original city plan of Buenos Aires on a piece of cowhide. A popular gaucho game—*taba* —involves throwing a piece of cow bone and betting on which side will face up when it lands. *Carne* in other Spanish-speaking countries means meat in general but in Argentina it means just one thing: beef.

Argentines have always been insatiable carnivores thanks to the abundant cattle herds that have roamed the pampas ever since Pedro de Mendoza's ill-fated expedition in 1536. Argentine cattle have kept the domestic market well supplied with beef since colonial times and there has always been plenty left over to export abroad. South of the Río Colorado, where the lush grasslands of the pampas turn into the plains of Patagonia, cattle are swapped for sheep, and in the kitchen, lamb largely replaces beef.

Given such enormous quantities of meat, at only a fraction of the price it would cost in other countries, Argentines cook it in the most sensible way—hurling it onto grills over hot coals and open fires in the greatest of all Argentine institutions—the *asado*.

The Ultimate Beef Fest

The *asado* is a wildly popular Argentine barbecue, which involves the consumption of enormous quantities of meat,

Keep an eye out for *chimichurri*, a spicy hot sauce made with herbs, oil and vinegar. Its name is rumoured to have come from English immigrants demanding 'give me curry'. It won't burn the roof of your mouth off but in a world of steak and salad it adds a welcome spicy punch.

sloshed down with gallons of red wine in the company of friends and family. Practically every house with a garden or patio will have a *parrilla* (the grill for making the *asado*) and every Argentine knows how to throw a wonderful *asado* party. The rules are simple: the men cook the meat and the women make the salad. It's a macho rule but one that everyone seems perfectly happy with. It is a matter of pride to the Argentine male that he gets his *asado* going without any help or suggestions from others, particularly—heaven forbid—a woman. I once observed a man in Salta surreptitiously resorting to his girlfriend's hairdryer to keep the flames alight.

Those unfortunate enough to have to work on the weekends—the classic *asado* time—won't go without their meat fix either. Even in urban centres, impromptu sizzling barbecues are set up on the roadside next to potholes and pneumatic drills, or in the middle of dusty building sites. Hard hats momentarily cast aside, everyone congregates around the *parrilla* and tucks into the usual vast quantities of meat.

Instead of attending an outdoor barbecue, Argentines may flock to a *parrilla*, an Argentine steakhouse. Here, the meat is still cooked over open coals, but this time by an *asador*. The *asador* is something of a local hero. He is normally a bear of a man who swelters over the *parrilla*, stoking the coals with one hand and battering out hunks of beef and entrails with the other. It is he (and believe me, it's always a he) whom we must thank for cooking the meat to perfection.

The main cuts of beef are *bife de chorizo* (a thick juicy rump steak cut off the rib), *bife de lomo* (sirloin), *bife de costilla* (T-bone steak), *tira de asado* (strip of rib) and *vacio* (a flavoursome cut similar to sirloin). Don't miss out on the *matambre* either. This is a flank steak stuffed with boiled eggs and vegetables, rolled up and usually served cold. If you like your beef rare, ask for it *jugoso*; if you want it well done then ask for *bien hecho*; medium-cooked is *a punto*.

Machismo even dominates Argentine cuisine, as seen of this *asador* manning the *parilla*.

Served alongside these enormous steaks are even more meaty titbits.

Practically every bit of the cow is eaten in Argentina, including all its innards and entrails, tongue and tail. Argentines, however, draw the line at lungs. Assorted offaly accompaniments include *chinchulines* (small intestines), also known affectionately as *chinchis*, which are served with lemon and surprisingly popular among women; *tripa gorda* (large intestines); *ubre* (udder); *riñones* (kidneys); *corazon* (heart); *higado* (liver); *mollejas* (sweetbreads); *lengua* (tongue)—best cooked in vinegar; *sesos* (brain); *chorizo* (spicy pork sausage); and *morcilla* (rich blood sausage), which tastes wonderful pasted onto bread as an appetiser.

If you order the *parrillada*, you will get all of these piled on a sizzling hot plate brought to your table along with juicy cuts of beef (and chicken and lamb, if you so wish). And don't miss out on a hunk of *provoletta*, a delectable golden cheese melted and sizzled over

Beefy Eaters

Argentines eat on average an astounding 59 kg (130 pounds) of beef each per year.

Typical Argentine Dishes

- *empanadas*—meat or cheese patties
- pizza
- various pasta dishes including *tallarines* (fettuccine), *ñoquis* (gnocchi), and *canelones* (cannelloni)
- *sandwiches de miga*—ham and cheese sandwiches made with thinly sliced, crustless white bread
- *tortilla*—onion and potato omelette
- *choripán*—spicy sausage in crusty baguette
- *parrillada*—mixed grill
- *bife de chorizo*—the finest rump steak you will ever eat
- *bife a caballo* – beefsteak topped with two fried eggs
- *matambre*—rolled flank steak filled with vegetables, eggs and herbs
- *arroz con pollo*—chicken with rice
- *milanesa*—breaded and fried meat (schnitzel)
- *milanesa completa*—milanesa with fried eggs and French fries
- *sorrentinos*—large, round ravioli stuffed with mozzarella, ricotta and basil in a tomato sauce
- *carbonada*—regional meat stew with beef, corn and pumpkin
- *locro*—corn and meat stew
- *puchero*—Spanish-style meat and vegetable stew
- *chivito*—goat
- *centolla*—king crab
- *cordero patagónico*—Patagonian lamb
- *buseca*—a tripe and vegetable soup
- *lechón*—suckling pig
- *lengua a la vinagreta*—tongue in vinegar
- *pionono*—a sort of swiss roll with a savoury filling
- *salpicón*—a cold vegetable and meat salad
- *flan*—caramel custard
- *tocino del cielo*—a rich, creamy egg and sugar dessert
- *torta galesa*—welsh cake, a type of fruit bread
- *mazamorra*—corn pudding
- *arroz con leche*—rice pudding
- *panqueques de dulce de leche*—caramel crepes
- *anchi*—a cornflour and citrus fruit dessert
- *queso y dulce*—cheese and quince jam
- *helado*—ice cream

the *parrilla*. Unless you're extraordinarily hungry, don't even think about tackling one of these on your own. Bring some friends, preferably a rugby team, along with you.

SOMETHING FISHY?

If you think that Argentina's 5,000 km (3,107 miles) of coastline should throw up all sorts of tasty seafood dishes, you're in for a shock. Although Argentina is a big fish producer and exporter, Argentines on the whole are not big fish eaters. There are, however, a few fishy surprises in store that shouldn't be missed if they come your way. The first is centolla, a spectacular king crab and a specialty from Tierra del Fuego, where it is scooped out of the Beagle Channel. It is also eagerly gobbled up by the neighbouring Chileans—big seafood eaters. Also keep your eyes open for pejerrey, a great fish from inland rivers and lakes, as well as the dorado and the monstrous surubi catfish—both caught in the rivers of the northeast.

When eating or ordering seafood always take local advice. The red tide (*marea roja*) periodically affects shellfish in the area with deadly results.

... AND SOMETHING SWEET

Argentines have a notoriously sweet tooth, so it was obvious that they would invent *dulce de leche* sooner or later. This sticky, decadent concoction of caramelised milk is an Argentine classic and can be bought in tubs from supermarkets and corner shops throughout the country. It is a standard spread for bread, croissants and cakes and is used in much the same way that the rest of us use jam or marmalade. There is also *dulce de leche* flavoured ice cream, *dulce de leche* flavoured yogurt and custard cream topped with *dulce de leche*. When Argentines travel abroad, *dulce de leche* is often one of the things they miss most—along with beef, tango and *mate*.

Obviously *dulce de leche* creations have a monopoly on the dessert menus, but other popular desserts are custard cream (*flan*), fruit salad (*ensalada de fruta*), ice cream (*helado*) and the very Argentine *queso con dulce*, which is a gooey cheese

served with quince jam (*dulce de membrillo*) or with sweet potato jam (*dulce de batata*).

DINING OUT

When they are not crowded around their kitchen table like members of a large Sicilian family—incessant chatter over forkfuls of spaghetti flying this way and that—or tucking into a wonderful *asado* in their garden, Argentines love to eat out. Even in times of economic straits everybody eats out as often as they possibly can, even if it's only a trip to the local pizzeria on the corner.

Cities and towns are geared towards a restaurant and café culture. Strolling around any plaza or down a main street, the visitor can spot, through café windows, thousands of shiny forks diving into bowls of pasta, slices of pizza held aloft, glistening ice creams, crumbling croissants and gooey pastries being licked off sticky fingers.

Eating Hours

Dinner is probably the main meal of the day, with lunch coming a close second. Sometimes this is reversed: big lunch, small dinner. Mind you, Argentines are quite capable of sitting down to a hearty meal at both, accompanied by gallons of the local wine and finished off with powerful espressos. Breakfast, on the other hand, is a non-event. At its most extravagant, it is a standard fare of *media lunas* (croissants) and coffee, but more often than not it is just a *café con leche* (a large milky coffee) or a shared *mate*. They have, you must remember, probably just stepped off the dance floor and a light breakfast rounds off the night nicely.

There are no rigid rules for when you can or cannot eat. Cafés and *confiterías* (larger, elegant and slightly old-fashioned cafés) are open throughout the day and well into the night—often all night. *Café con leche* and croissants are still served at three in the afternoon and you can order a toasted ham and cheese sandwich at 4:00 am should you so wish. Restaurants, on the other hand, will open for lunch, close during the afternoon and open again in the late evening for dinner.

Lunch takes place at about 1:00 pm. It may last several hours or be just a frantic sandwich grabbed while you can. Don't even think about going out for dinner, however, until at least 9:00 pm—and even that's considered early. Argentines eat late. When most restaurants throughout the rest of the world are wiping down their tables and bidding a weary farewell to their last customers, Argentines are just tucking into their first course and cracking open the *vino*. Ten, eleven, even midnight is a perfectly normal time to sit down to dinner. Even in the smallest of provincial towns, it's considered abnormal to go out for supper before 9:00 pm. (Nothing will be open anyway.) The same rules apply if you're eating in.

With at least eight hours between lunch and dinner, teatime is crucial. At 5:00 pm, cafés start filling up and orders are put in for more coffee and cake. This is the perfect time to eat *facturas*—delicious pastries stuffed with that old faithful, *dulce de leche*. Teatime is also a popular time to meet friends at home. If you are invited to someone's house for tea, do pop into a bakery on your way and bring a bag of *facturas* along with you.

Ordering

Waiters will respond to *camarero*, *che*, *mozo*, *flaco* and just about any other Argentine nickname, but you won't have to make much effort to get their attention as they are incredibly on the ball. Table waiting is a noble occupation in Argentina and customer service is generally impeccable. In the more traditional *confiterías*, waiters are invariably ancient men in bow ties and stiff white aprons with surprisingly steady hands. Occasionally, you can't help feeling as if your grandfather is serving you and that perhaps you ought to leap up and help. But once you've seen Argentine waiters in action—young and old alike—you soon realise that you are in the hands of experts.

Just ordering a small espresso in a café becomes a mesmerising event. In a flurry of hands and silver trays, the waiter will deposit a napkin, a coaster, an ashtray, a complimentary glass of soda water, a plate of macaroons, white packets of sugar, pink packets of artificial sweetener, your coffee and finally the bill, skewered majestically onto a metal spike. The entire process takes just a few seconds. He deserves a round of applause, not to mention a tip.

For meals in restaurants, the bill won't be brought to you until you have finished your meal and asked for it. This is done by raising your hand and moving it around, as if you were writing in the air. But don't feel you have to rush. Argentines spend hours at the table, lingering over coffee after coffee, deep in discussion. Traditionally, this is a time when the whole family gathers together and discusses anything and everything. Waiters respect this tradition—known locally as the *sobremesa*—and won't boot you out to make space for new customers just because you've finished eating.

The only time a waiter's role becomes fairly redundant is at a *tenedor libre* restaurant. For a set price of about US$ 3 to US$ 4, *tenedor libres* (literally, 'free fork') let you eat as much as you want from an open buffet. This is wonderful value if you're especially hungry. Needless to say, they are exceptionally popular among gangs of ravenous young men who, much to the disdain of the restaurateur, manage to polish off more than their fair share of the goodies on offer.

FOOD SHOPPING

Most Argentines buy the bulk of their food from supermarkets, which are well stocked and found everywhere. These are wonderful enclaves for all sorts of Italian goodies such as pizza, mozzarella, tomato sauces and Parmesan cheese. There are entire aisles devoted to different pasta types alone. Then, of course, there is the meat section, manned

Contented lunchtime diners reflected in a mirror of a Buenos Aires *parilla*.

by fierce-looking men in blood-spattered aprons, wielding hatchets. It's at the meat counter where you really do get an idea about the innards and offal that you've been happily gobbling at an *asado*. They don't make any effort to make these look pretty, and unless you have a strong stomach, steel yourself to see tongues hacked up and intestines unravelled in front of you. Supermarkets are also often the best—and cheapest—places to buy wine and other drinks but the fruit and vegetable sections often look as if they could do with some cheering up. For these you're best off going to the specialist fresh fruit and vegetable stalls— usually cleverly located directly opposite the supermarket. In smaller towns, look out for fruit and vegetable wagons that are pulled around the streets. Likewise, supermarkets generally have a good bakery section, but for a greater selection and variety of breads and pastries go to a *panadería* (bakery).

Home delivery is also popular, especially for pizzas and *empanadas*. The deliverymen travel to your front door by motorbike, and in a land of motoring maniacs are some of the most dangerous on the road. They will expect a tip.

DRINK

Argentines guzzle gallons of soft drinks. The standard cola, diet cola and lemonade are everywhere but do look out for the local tonic water, *Paso de los Toros*, which also comes in a fizzy grapefruit (*pomelo*) flavour. And you won't be able to miss the local beer, *Quilmes*, which comes in cans and litre bottles.

The cheapest soft drink to order in a bar or restaurant is soda water. This normally arrives in old-fashioned soda bottles with metal or plastic siphons. Make sure you get the right pressure and angle when squeezing the handle. If not, you can easily soak yourself and your companions. Tap water is generally drinkable everywhere in Argentina but if you're worried or have a very sensitive stomach ask for mineral water—either fizzy (*agua con gas*) or still (*agua sin gas*).

All these drinks, however, come leagues behind in the popularity stakes after wine, coffee and *yerba mate*.

> ### Snacking
>
> Considering the enormous gap between lunch at about 1:00 pm and dinner some nine or ten hours later (and often no breakfast at all), snacking is not only an enjoyable Argentine tradition but one that is essential to survival. The most readily available snack to knock those hunger pains on the head is the *alfajor*, a crumbly thick biscuit sandwich filled with the eternally popular *dulce de leche* and bathed in chocolate. The smarter varieties often come coated in meringue.
>
> Entire dynasties have been founded on the humble *alfajor*. Like fudge or rock in other counties, each region produces its own unique brand of *alfajor* and in practically every town throughout the country, you can buy your *alfajores* with quaint pictures of the local scenery on the box. It is also considered the perfect goodwill gesture and an ideal gift to bring your hostess.
>
> Other snacks include the handy *empanada*, a cheese or meat patty stuffed with olives and hardboiled egg, prodigious in the northwest and popular everywhere else. *Choripán* is a delicious spicy sausage split open and sandwiched between thick crusty white bread and available from every roadside stall. *Pancho* is the local term for a hot dog, a super *pancho* being an enormous hot dog. When winter starts to kick in, don't miss out on *churros con chocolate*. *Churros* are long, fat, deep-fried doughy sticks, decadently stuffed with—you guessed it—*dulce de leche*, and the hot chocolate's so thick you can stand both your spoon—and the *churro*—up in it.
>
> Meanwhile, if you want something to nibble on with your cold drink in a café ask the waiter for a *picada*—he or she will conjure up a small plate of crisps, nuts and olives.

Yerba Mate

Mate (pronounced 'mah-tay') is a tea made from the leaves and stems of the *yerba mate* bush, which is related to holly and grows like a weed in the Paraná and Paraguay river basins. Its scientific name is *Ilex paraguarensis*, and it is also known as Paraguayan tea and Jesuit tea—apparently Jesuit missionaries in the 18th century were quite hooked on *mate* after being introduced to it by Guaraní Indians. In

Argentina, however, it is always referred to as either *yerba mate* or simply *mate*.

Mate is a well-kept secret—it is commonly drunk only in Argentina, Paraguay, Uruguay and southern Brazil. Yet among the various merits of *I. paraguarensis* are its properties as a stimulant to the central nervous system, a diuretic, an anti-rheumatic and a tonic. In extremely large doses it causes purging and vomiting. Some herbalists have gone so far as to suggest that it can delay the signs of ageing (even stop you from going grey), reduce stress and stimulate your mind. One Argentine acquaintance that swears by its seduction potential gives girlfriends the ultimation, "Darling, either we drink *mate* or go to bed." I guess sooner or later the poor girl has to give in or OD.

One thing's certain: *mate* drinking keeps the Argentines permanently on their toes. The active ingredient in *mate* is a powerful little alkaloid known as mateine, which, to all intents and purposes, is identical to caffeine and packs the same punch. Here may well lie the secret of Argentines' ability to party night after night and be the key to becoming a true *trasnochador*.

Mate plays a key part in Argentine culture and at times you could be forgiven for thinking that the entire country is happily hooked on this mildly narcotic tea. The vast majority of Argentines won't go anywhere without their *mate* and a thermos flask for a ready supply of hot water. They are quick to point out, however, that they are not nearly as addicted as their friends in Uruguay, where the locals are quite capable of drinking *mate* and riding their bicycles at the same time, a thermos flask neatly tucked under their arm.

Still, most Argentines drink *mate* several times a day—as many as eight times a day in the countryside. To say that the Argentines love their *mate* is no exaggeration. There's even been tangos written about it—and in Argentina that's about as high an accolade as you can get.

Drinking the Stuff

A wooden gourd (also confusingly known as a *mate*) is stuffed with *yerba mate* and filled with hot, but never boiling or boiled, water. The resulting tea is drunk through a metal, often silver, straw known as a *bombilla*. At first, this strikes you as ludicrous as the water that's poured into the *mate* is just off boiling point and the *bombilla* quickly gets red hot and sticks to your lower lip. It may even give the inexperienced *mate* drinker a blister. Once you get the knack, by which time you'll probably be as addicted as the next Argentine, you won't want to drink it any cooler. (Although Paraguayans, and some Argentines from the north, drink their *mate* ice-cold, as *tereré*—much to the amusement and horror of the rest of Argentina.)

Yerba mate can be bought in kilos everywhere in Argentina under various brand names. A kilo should keep a family of four happily wired for about a week. Essential *mate* drinking paraphernalia—a thermos flask (to store the hot water), a *bombilla* and the *mate* gourd—can be purchased cheaply in supermarkets and thrift stores throughout the country. Some *bombillas* and *mates* can be very elaborate affairs: ornate silver-plated antique mates and *bombillas* can fetch hundreds of dollars. *Mates* also come in all sorts of different shapes and sizes. They are made from calabashes, aromatic wood and even out of bull's testicles.

Drinking *mate* is a very social affair; mate is usually drunk among friends and family gathered together at home. One *mate* is passed round and round a group. Each person drinks the full serving before passing it back to be refilled by the 'server', who then passes it on again. As you can imagine, the mateine kick sparks up the already chatty Argentines no end. It's an endless circle—the more *mate* you drink the more you talk, and the more you talk the longer you stay drinking mate.

For these reasons alone, you should never turn down an opportunity to drink *mate*. But be warned—the first time you try it, however adventurous your taste buds are, you'll probably find it revolting. "It always tastes like someone's spat into it," said one acquaintance. "It was like putting my lips round an exhaust pipe," said another about the *bombilla*. Unaccustomed drinkers have described *mate* as tasting like earth, bonfire smoke, withered

Rows of *mate* gourds ready for use.

leaves and boiled straw. One visitor thought that they were doing drugs.

The best advice is to persevere and you should come to love and revere it as much as the Argentines. In the process you will provide your hosts with lots of amusement at the vision of a gringo drinking *mate*. Personally, after months of perseverance, I'm now as hooked as the next Argentine and can't contemplate a day without a *mate* hit.

Mate Etiquette

The *mate* ritual is rather reminiscent of a Native American peace pipe ceremony. An offer of *mate* is a sign of friendship and to be included in a round of *mate* means that you have been accepted. No self-respecting Argentine would dream of drinking *mate* on his own without offering it around to everyone else in the room. If an Argentine offers you a *mate* you may feel that you can congratulate yourself on having got this far.

But don't sit back and relax just yet. An amazing and intricate set of rules and regulations revolves around the art of *mate* drinking. Commit a *mate faux pas* now and you could blow your chances at impressing your new friends— not to mention becoming a laughing stock.

The first thing you should be aware of is saying, or rather not saying, thank you. Most of us when offered a drink will automatically be inclined to thank our host. But if you thank an Argentine who has just handed you a *mate*, it will be taken as a 'no thank you'. You will be excluded from the next round and may end up feeling left out. If you really feel that you can't just accept a drink without saying something, try murmuring an appreciative comment instead, perhaps something like 'yum, how delicious' or 'great *mate* this'. But never say thank you, unless of course you don't want any more.

Once you have accepted a *mate*, you will be expected to drink all of it. There's no room for half-hearted measures in the *mate* ritual. The problem, however, is that you will probably take one mouth-scalding boiled straw sip and your instinct will be to hand it back quickly to wherever it came from. To do so would be to commit a grave social blunder, akin to giving someone your mangy leftovers. You will know when you have drunk all the liquid because the *bombilla* will make a loud gurgling slurpy noise as you come to the end—it should sound rather like the noise that is made as you suck up the dregs of a milkshake through a straw. Only once you've made the 'milkshake slurp' can you pass the *mate* back.

This leads us to another potential *mate* minefield. Faced with the prospect of having to down the entire blisteringly hot drink in one fell swoop, you may be tempted to play for time in the hope that the drink will cool off or someone will take it away from you—basically doing anything to distract from the matter in hand. This is considered awfully bad manners. One should never 'sit' on the *mate* for too long; ideally you should finish the entire drink in as few slurps as possible without ever putting it down on the table and quickly hand it back to your host. (Some *mates* are designed with a round bottom so that they cannot be put down.) By sitting on the mate, you become a '*mate* hog' and are not entering into the spirit of the *mate* ritual.

Occasionally, in a futile attempt to cool down the *mate*, unaccustomed mate drinkers play around with the *bombilla*. Don't be tempted! The *bombilla* stays put, whatever. On no account should you pull it out or, worse still, try and stir the *mate*. Should you do so, you will be greeted by horrified gasps and the *mate* will be snatched away from you immediately, as if you were a small toddler making icky messes with his food.

Once you finish the *mate*, you should always hand it back to the *cebador* (the person who prepared the *mate*), who will then refill it and pass it on to the next person in the round.

Preparing *Mate*

The *matero*, or any keen *mate* drinker, should have the art of preparing a *mate* down to a T. Here are seven pointers that should turn you into an ace *matero*:

- Fill the *mate* (gourd) to about two-thirds full with *yerba mate*.
- Cover the top of the *mate* with your hand and shake it gently upside down. This forces the smaller particles to the top so that they don't get sucked up and clog the *bombilla*.
- Pour hot water (around 80°C), never boiling or boiled water, gently into the *mate* at the edge of the gourd near the *bombilla*, until it rises to the top. If you've done it right, a froth should cover the surface.
- Let the *mate* stand a few seconds. It may need a little top-up the first time as the dry *mate* leaves absorb the water. But be careful not to overfill.
- Close the *bombilla*'s mouthpiece with your thumb and insert it firmly into the *mate*. From now on, do not move it again, play with it or pull it out even when refilling with water. And never stir.
- If you prepare the *mate*, you must take the first drink, which is normally very bitter and strong. As the *cebador*, it will be your duty to refill the *mate* with water each time and pass it on.
- If the *mate* loses its foaminess and you can see little bits of stalk floating on the surface, then your mate is *lavado* (washed) and will have lost its taste. To avoid a mate becoming *lavado*—which will happen eventually if you go a lot of rounds—add a little more *yerba mate* every three or four servings.

Drinking *mate* is an acquired taste and requires much practice.

Curing and Caring for Your Mate

If you buy a brand new *mate* gourd—which is likely as an Argentine will be reluctant to part with his—your *mate* just won't taste the same until your gourd's been weathered, or cured. To do this, you must fill your newly purchased gourd with used *yerba mate*, add hot water and let it stand for a day. The next day remove all the *mate*, rinse the gourd and scrape out any soft tissue. Repeat the whole process. You may need to do this for several days. As long as you're still scraping out soft tissue, your gourd is not completely cured and any *mate* served in it will taste unusually bitter.

It is a cardinal sin to clean your gourds with detergent; the *mate* would be tainted with a soapy flavour for weeks. Simply rinse out the *mate* with cold water and let it stand to dry. *Bombillas* should be cleaned regularly so that the sieve-like end doesn't become clogged with little particles. Many *bombillas* can be dismantled to make cleaning easier.

Strangely enough, despite its universal popularity, you won't be able to order a *mate* in a restaurant or café. The closest you can get is a *mate cocido*, which is *mate* leaves in a tea bag. Cafés are normally reserved for the second national drink: coffee.

Café Society

When it comes to caffeine consumption, the Argentines are unbeatable. Decaffeinated coffee is practically unheard of and there's even a popular brand of aspirin—*cafiaspirina*—which is laced with high quantities of caffeine and boldly claims to soothe headaches, combat colds and boost your spirits all at the same time.

In the quest to be spiced with caffeine, Argentines across the country have perfected coffee houses into an art form. You must also remember that this is a nationality that simply adores chatting, and what could be nicer than chatting over steaming coffee in one of Argentina's justifiably famous cafés?

Argentine society is a café society at heart, and a great deal of time is spent dawdling over cups of coffee in the country's cafés and *confiterías*. There is at least one café on the corner of each block and usually a few more in between. If you want to meet up with someone, you arrange a rendezvous not at the office or on a street corner, but in a café. As a result, cafés are generally packed throughout the day and well into the night. It's also totally acceptable to sit on your own in a café at any time of the day or night—no pitying looks will be forthcoming and you'll be left in peace.

After all, cafés are there to be sat in. It's practically impossible to get a coffee in a polystyrene cup to 'take away'. You can, however, order a coffee to be brought to your office. An efficient waiter will leave the café, cross the street and serve you coffee in a proper cup on a silver tray at your desk, then return and take away the cup once you've finished.

Coffee comes in all sorts of varieties, the most popular being the *café cortado*—a lethally strong espresso cut with a shot of steamed milk. Argentines like their coffee sweet and will heap up to five spoonfuls of sugar into a coffee cup that is marginally larger than a thimble. If you take your coffee unsweetened, brace yourself for some bemused looks. As well as the *cortado*, there are cappuccinos (which come topped with cream and chocolate powder), espressos (black and potent) and *café con leche*—a large milky coffee that's ideal at breakfast. Most coffees arrive with a complimentary glass of soda water and little macaroon-like biscuits.

Suffice to say, caffeine consumption, be it from mate, coffee or *cafiaspirina*, keeps most Argentines wired most of the time.

WINE

Just as they are hugely proud of their *bife*, Argentines are also prone to bragging that they produce some of the best wine in the world, and to prove it (until very recently) they drank it all themselves. By the late 1970s the average Argentine was putting away an astonishing 91 litres (96 quarts) of wine a year.

Thanks to this insatiable domestic market, for many years Argentina found itself with nothing left over to export. But all this is changing. Argentina is now

There are enough bottles of *vino* in this *bodega* to keep its customers happy for weeks!

the fourth largest producer of wine in the world and although local consumption is still considerable (today Argentines boast the world's third largest per capita consumption of wine), there's a lot more Argentine wine entering the international market.

Not that this needs to concern you if you are actually in Argentina and have joined the ranks of the happy domestic wine-guzzling market, where you can pick up a decent bottle of *vino* for little more than a dollar.

Choosing a Wine

Argentine wines range from the very good to extremely rough, and if you don't have any local guidance, buying wine can turn into a bit of a lottery. Still, when a bottle of wine can cost the same as a litre of cola, the key is experimentation.

Wines in Argentina are divided into two categories: noble wines or fine wines known as *vino fino* and cheaper table wines known as *vino comun* or *vino de mesa*.

By law, only *vino fino* can be put into the small three-quarter litre bottles. *Vino comun* goes into litre bottles or boxes, and into the phenomenal five-litre containers.

Whether an Argentine wine is *comun* or *fino* has nothing to do with the price—although *vino fino* is generally more expensive and *vino comun* can be as cheap as US$ 0.50 a bottle. Rather it has to do with the type of grape from which the wine is made. There are very strict regulations as to what grapes can be used in different areas of the country for different types of wine.

You also won't find a *vino comun* which is varietal—in other words made from one single type of grape. It will usually be a mixture of fairly cheap grapes to make a cheap wine.

Grape varieties grown in Argentina include Malbec, Torrontés, Chardonnay, Chenin, Riesling, Sauvignon, Cabernet Sauvignon and Merlot. But it's really the Malbec (a red) and the Torrontés (a white) that are taking the world by storm.

The Vineyards

Argentina's vineyards flourish in the Mendoza region—which produces over 70 per cent of all Argentine wines—but there are also vineyards in San Juan, Salta, La Rioja and Río Negro provinces. Argentina takes full advantage of the extraordinarily dry climate throughout the Andean region which allows just the right amount of humidity and water that the vines need. A further plus for Argentine wines is that they are made from very natural, clean and healthy grapes. In a bad year, grapes are only sprayed twice, compared with 10 or 12 times in Chile and even more in Brazil.

Quite a number of vineyards and wineries (*bodegas*) are well worth a visit and all will welcome you with open arms and bottles. To mention just a couple, try Chandon, with its fantastic sparkling wine installation, or Norton's picturesque old-style winery, both in Mendoza. For a more picturesque and exotic setting, visit the vineyards in the whitewashed colonial-style town of Cafayate, Salta.

ENJOYING THE CULTURE

CHAPTER 7

'Boca is my heart's joy. You're my life; you're my passion,
more than anything. It doesn't matter where you play, I'll
come and see you at home or away. Not even death will
separate us, I'll support you from heaven.'
—Boca Juniors football song

A FOOTBALL-MAD NATION

Football is, without doubt, what really drives the Argentines to fever pitch. Forget Mass or even a famous death, this is Argentina's universal religion. Football players acquire an almost godlike status. Top players and team managers form a key part of Argentina's *farándula* or jet set, often dating models and actresses. In fact, Argentine football players are stars in their own right—Diego Maradona's sex, drugs and rock 'n' roll antics have kept the paparazzi in business for years.

In Argentina, football (soccer to North Americans) is more of an institution than just a game. No one can be a mere passive spectator. Fans tend to strip to the waist (male ones anyway) and paint their faces in their team's colours. Flares, firecrackers, smoke bombs and gunpowder along with endless singing all create stupendous noise levels, while streams of tickertape are hurled down from the stands onto the pitch below. Often tear gas and plastic bullets are added to the general commotion by police stationed to keep things under control. Some of the more fanatical supporters go armed with knives and guns, which they aren't afraid to whip out should they encounter the opposition. In fact, as one cynical commentator put it, "Argentina is one of the few countries in the world where people are prepared to kill each other over a game."

Key games are often brought forward to Friday and Saturday evenings—as well as the ubiquitous Sunday afternoon slot—for optimum televised viewing. During these

times all eyes not in the stadium itself are lovingly glued to TV screens. And you can't escape the fervour over a quiet *café con leche* down the street. Every cantina and café throughout the country will also be showing the game at top volume with the customers letting out huge synchronised cheers when their team scores a goal or even rushing out onto the sidewalk to let off fireworks and ear-splitting bangers. If the game has been particularly spectacular, fans will take to the streets in their hordes, banging drums or driving round and round the plaza honking their car horns.

This obsession with football is encouraged from an early age. A football is generally the first toy a baby boy is given, usually when he's just a few months old. By the time they've reached school age, many boys dream of playing one day for a premier division team or, better still, the national squad. "For practically all Argentine boys, football is a madness and playing is the thing that interests them the most," says José-Luis Barrios, a commentator at *El Gráfico* sports magazine. "It's the most popular sport in the country by far. It's an Argentine passion."

No open space is left unused. Empty car lots are transformed into impromptu football pitches at the weekends, lamp posts double up as goal posts and the walls of telephone booths become heated arenas of a graffiti war between various teams. It is no exaggeration to say that Argentine men literally spend hours talking about football. If you pass a group of guys deep in conversation you can bet that it's probably not about girls, cars or even pizza. They will be talking football. This leads to the popular local saying that wives don't have husbands on Sunday afternoons. Mind you, I've also known women to drop everything when a River-Boca game comes on television.

El Clásico: Boca vs River

Two teams dominate Argentina's cutthroat football scene: Boca Juniors and River Plate, better known as just 'Boca' and 'River'. Both teams are from Buenos Aires, which has undoubtedly intensified the legendary rivalry. And even if you support another team for the rest of the year, when these two battle it out on the pitch, you're going to take sides. The fanaticism is infectious.

A Boca-River game is known as *El Clásico*—'The Classic' —and it's easy to see why. As equally matched archenemies, a game between these two giants temporarily splits the country in two. Between them, Boca and River can claim almost two-thirds of the country as fans. A recent study revealed that 32 per cent of Argentines support Boca, and 30 per cent are River fans.

But it's the Boca Junior fan that is the most vociferous and passionate. '*La mitad mas uno*'—'half the country plus one,' say Boca fans about the supporters. And although this is not strictly true, judging by noise levels alone, you may at times believe it. Many Boca fans come from the same background as their former star player, Diego Maradona, whose family were poor immigrants. For them, football is an escape valve, something to believe in. Their home ground is the square-shaped Bombonera stadium in the traditionally working-class Italian neighbourhood of La Boca. *Bombonera* means 'chocolate box' in Spanish but, as writer Jimmy Burns points out, "there is nothing sweet or contained about the scene." When there's lots of singing and stamping—as is usual practice—the whole stadium shakes.

Exitable Boca fans during a football match.

River fans may be marginally quieter than Boca's, but are equally fond of chucking tickertape and letting off fireworks and are no less fanatical. As my friend Juan Luciano, a keen River supporter, pointed out, "If I have a son and he supports Boca, I'll disinherit him."

Bad Losers and Hooligans

What makes Argentina's football scene stand out so much more than other Latin countries', which are also known for their extreme passion for the game, are the highly organised

At the other end of the stadium, River fans unite to show their support for their favourite team.

and violent hooligan groups known as the *barra bravas* lurking behind the scenes. The *barra bravas* are the Argentine equivalent of football hooligans but are even more sinister in that they are seemingly above the law, despite being blatantly involved in drug-dealing, intimidation and even murder. In short, they're a nasty bunch.

"We all know who they are," says Barrios from *El Gráfico*. "They go to the stadiums with drugs and weapons. In a multitude of 40,000 or 50,000 they are no more than 200 or 300 but that's enough to cause conflict."

The *barra bravas* are there to do the dirty work. Club leaders may owe them favours or ask favours of them. The *barra bravas* act as the 'heavies'. For example, club leaders may encourage their *barra bravas* to threaten those who want to participate in club elections against them. They use them as personal bodyguards or to stick up posters. It's not unheard of for the *barra bravas* to go to a training session and threaten players of their own team who are playing badly or intimidate a trainer into resignation. At games, they are the fiercest supporters, often armed with knives, guns or just sheer brute force. They're largely responsible for selling drugs in the stands, robbery and even nastier crimes.

Violence at football matches is becoming an increasing concern for the authorities. (At one stage all second division matches were temporarily banned by a judge because he thought that the violence had got out of control.) One sad result is that women and young children are now quite a rare sight at football matches.

Surviving a Football Match

Given this powerful and intimidating combination of the bloodthirsty *barra bravas* and a general atmosphere that borders on mass hysteria, you may think twice before rushing off to see a football match. Still, if you do decide to go—and if you really want to get to grips with Argentine culture, you should experience at least one match—take note of the following pointers and try to tag along with someone local who'll know the scene.

- Jump when everyone else jumps. Concentrate on staying on your feet at all times and don't lose your balance. "It was the closest thing to a heavy metal mosh pit I've come across since I've lived in Argentina," said a Californian friend about a Racing vs Huracán match he'd seen. "If you don't jump when everyone else does, you're going to get trampled."
- Seats or stands? Seats (*plateas*) are safer than stands (*populares*) and more expensive. But it's in the stands where the passion is really felt. You decide.
- Leave your valuables at home. Don't tempt fate and wear an expensive watch or jewellery or, for that matter, bring your wallet along with you, just enough cash to see you back home.
- Stick to neutral colours. You don't want to be the only one wearing blue in a sea of red.

Decked out in the country's national colours, this Argentine football fan shows support for his country.

Argentina's Top 20 Teams and Their Colours

- Argentinos Juniors (Buenos Aires)—all red
- Boca Juniors (Buenos Aires)—yellow/dark blue
- Belgrano (Córdoba)—light blue
- Colón (Santa Fe)—half black, half red
- Estudiantes (La Plata)—red and white stripes
- Ferrocarril Oeste (Buenos Aires)—green
- Gimnasia y Esgrima (Jujuy)—white and light blue
- Gymnasio (La Plata)—white and dark blue
- Huracán (Buenos Aires)—white with red collar
- Independiente (Buenos Aires)—all red
- Lanus (Buenos Aires)—burgundy
- Newell's Old Boys (Rosario)—half black, half red like Colón
- Platense (Buenos Aires)—white with dark brown stripes
- Racing Club (Buenos Aires)—light blue and white stripes (like the national colours)
- River Plate (Buenos Aires)—white with diagonal red stripe
- Rosario Central (Rosario)—yellow and blue stripes
- San Lorenzo (Buenos Aires)—blue and red vertical stripes
- Talleres (Córdoba)—dark blue and white vertical stripes
- Unión (Santa Fe)—red and white stripes
- Vélez Sarsfield (Buenos Aires)—white with blue 'V'

ANYONE FOR POLO?

Although polo didn't originate in Argentina, it is a sport that is unquestionably associated with the country and has been played here since 1875. Today, there are few polo teams in the world—good ones at least—that can't boast an Argentine player or two. Non-Argentines are invariably awestruck by the standard of Argentina's players, who, they joke, were probably born on a horse. It's not unusual to see small Argentine children fearlessly charging about on horseback clutching polo sticks while their contemporaries abroad have probably just mastered riding a bicycle. In fact, the local talent is so extensive that entire teams can be made up of brothers alone. (You can't help wondering if they were bred specifically for the purpose.)

Throughout the world, all polo players have a rating

A group of polo players on an *estancia* in the pampas.

known as a handicap, which reflects their ability and can range from zero goals for a complete beginner (minus two outside Argentina) up to a maximum of ten goals for the very best players. Argentina, understandably, holds the monopoly on the very best players. To get some idea of the Argentine talent, at the time of writing the best 27 polo players in the world are all Argentine. One of Argentina's best teams—formed by the dashing Heguy family—had, at one stage, a combined handicap of 40 goals, the absolute highest any team can get.

The Argentine polo player is frequently stereotyped as devilishly good-looking, devastatingly macho and usually to be seen with a martini in one hand and an exquisite girlfriend in the other. Chances are that he also rubs shoulders with Prince Charles and the Sultan of Brunei and has sponsors like Cartier. I know I shouldn't stereotype, but to be honest all the Argentine polo players I've met—male and female— were without exception unbelievably glamorous.

There are some polo players in Argentina who clearly lap up this attention, but many others are desperately trying to escape this image of the Argentine polo playboy. "They've got us wrong," said Marcial Socas over a glass of Coca-Cola in the kitchen of his *Estancia La Martina*. "We're quite normal really, we wear jeans and T-shirts—we're not that jet set."

True, the Argentine polo player may be marginally less affluent than his British or North American counterpart, and this is because polo is relatively much more financially accessible in Argentina than elsewhere. Still, you do need a certain amount of capital to indulge and therefore it's definitely a sport for Argentina's upper middle classes. "It's an expensive vice," polo players joke. In Argentina, a decent amateur polo pony goes for about US$ 4,000 (the same horse can easily fetch twice or even three times this amount when sold abroad). Of course any self-respecting polo player has at least four horses just to see him through the chukkers. Then there are the saddles, sticks, leather kneepads, helmets, gloves, balls, stable, stable hands, champagne and jet set lifestyle. It all adds up.

Should you decide to play polo, you will also have to devote hours talking shop with fellow polo fanatics. "All we ever do is talk about horses and polo the whole time," one player told me, barely dragging his eyes off the game we were watching together from the sidelines. "You decide if that's passionate or not."

If you visit a polo club or even an estancia while you are living in Argentina someone might well sidle up to you and ask, "Do you stick and ball?" In polo lingo, this means 'Do you know how to play polo?' (They'll probably ask you this in English as, among their many attributes, polo players also tend to be multi-lingual.) Answer 'yes' only if you're fairly good at polo. Argentine polo is played incredibly fast and the players are completely fearless. "If you fall off your horse in England, they'll probably call an ambulance," said Charlie, who spent a year polishing up his polo skills on an *estancia* outside Buenos Aires. "But here they are like, 'What are you doing down there on the ground? *Vamos*!" So unless, of course, you do 'stick and ball', you'll probably be much better off watching the game from the sidelines. As you'd imagine, polo involves a fair amount of unpleasant accidents and broken collarbones, even though practically all the rules are concerned with safety. A good polo player requires a certain devil-may-care attitude that must be rather appealing to the glamorous girlfriends on the sidelines.

Polo In A Nutshell

As a polo spectator, it's easy to get confused by the game. Put simply, two teams of four players try to hit a small wooden or plastic ball through two large goals at opposite ends of an enormous field. They are mounted on horses—polo ponies aren't ponies but fully-grown horses—and armed with wooden mallets, which they whirl ferociously through the air as they gallop across the pitch like wild dervishes. It all makes for a rather terrifying and invigorating spectacle.

All this lasts for seven frantic minutes, or a 'chukka'. After each chukka, the players race off the pitch, leap onto fresh mounts and start all over again. Matches last for between six and eight chukkas, depending on the standard of the players.

HITTING THE SLOPES

For many people, mountains mean skiing and in August thousands of Argentines with the means to indulge head for the slopes of the Andes. During this time of year the weather reports are avidly watched and the season's first heavy snowfall makes headline news across the country. If the snow reports look good you pack up and leave. Argentina's main ski resorts are Bariloche, Las Leñas, Chapelco (near San Martín de Los Andes) and the more isolated Ushuaia in Tierra del Fuego. Snow shortages and high winds can be a hindrance. "In Argentina you don't just say, let's go skiing this winter, you say, if there's snow, let's go skiing this winter," says Nico Busch, a member of the Argentine Ski Club.

What's more, Argentines don't go to these resorts just to ski; they go to party. There is probably not such a fantastic level of skiing as you might see in Europe. If the weather's bad, they wouldn't dream of stoically going out and braving it. They'd much rather stay in and drink hot chocolate, saving up their energy for a night of dancing. Likewise, if it's been a heavy night on the tiles, you stay in bed until your hangover's worn off. "I don't know of any other place in the world where skiers consistently go to bed at 6:00 am and get up in the afternoon," says Nico.

Country Houses

Distances are vast in Argentina, and Argentines don't think twice about travelling for hours for lunch or a social call. Some *estancias* (country estates) are so isolated that they have their own airstrips and petrol stations.

To combat this mileage problem, many *porteños* with the means to do so have sought out weekend cottages within 45 minutes' drive from downtown Buenos Aires. For convenience and safety, these *quintas* (country houses) are bunched together with other *quintas* in a secure enclosure. As one cynical commentator put it, "Everybody who lives together in the same Buenos Aires neighbourhood leaves Buenos Aires on Friday night and goes to another neighbourhood, where they spend the weekend 'getting away from it all' with the same people that they spent all week with."

These countryside enclosures are known as country clubs, or simply *los countries*. Most have a communal swimming pool, tennis courts and a brace of polo pitches. Security is tight: the area is surrounded by a fence and a mean-looking armed guard is posted at the gate. Not any old José can buy up and move into a country; you have to have your name put forward by a member.

Country clubs and private *barrios* may be heavily armed and closed off to the general public but in the real countryside it's relatively easy to stroll up to any rural *abode*. Should you decide to drop in on the residents of such establishments, it is customary to clap your hands together a couple of times as you approach. Many houses have open courtyards and visitors are few and far between, so if you don't make your arrival known beforehand you could spring your hosts in *flagrante*, or worse still, get attacked by their miffed Rottweiler. Many older people may also call out "*Ave Maria Purissima*" when approaching a house in the countryside.

TRUCO

It's a common sight to see duelling chess players engrossed over a game on a park bench or through a smoky café window. I'm quite convinced that the world's longest game of chess is taking place in a café in downtown Buenos Aires. Every time I walk past the window, two men—utterly absorbed in their game—are bent over a chessboard in unwavering concentration. They've been there for so long that the waiters treat them as part of the furniture, casually moving them to one side as they sweep the floor. But if you think they take chess seriously, you should see the Argentines get immersed in a game of *truco*.

Truco is a card game played with Spanish cards (depicting swords, cups, wands and pentacles as opposed to clubs, spades, hearts and diamonds) that involves much wit, a certain amount of skill and a natural ability to lie. The Argentine trait of *viveza criolla*—or artful lying—really comes into its own in a *truco* game. If it is played in pairs, as is usual, you are required to make certain facial expressions so that your partner sitting opposite can guess what you have in your hand. For example, a twitching cheek means you have a seven, a raised eyebrow and you're holding an ace. If you purse your lips you're probably holding a two. The real skill lies not so much in making the faces as in

If you really want to see the modern-day gauchos at their fearless best, try to get to a rodeo, known locally as a *doma* held throughout the country.

making them without the other pair seeing you. If they are watching closely, players may resort to playing footsie under the table, tapping messages across onto their partner's feet. Of course, all this is secondary to an ability to keep a poker face while lying through your teeth.

It will be well worth your while to learn how to play *truco* as long as you are in Argentina, although this is easier said than done. The rules are about as complicated and seemingly random as American football would be to an Englishman. Once you have learnt to play, however, you should not enter into a *truco* game lightly. *Truco* can be taken very seriously indeed and vast amounts of money have been known to change hands over games.

GAUCHO GAMES

Lots of original gaucho games are still played today in Argentina, the most flamboyant of which is *pato*, a sort of basketball crossed with rugby. Naturally, it is played on horseback and at great speed.

In the original form of the game, a duck—*pato* in Spanish—was put in a basket and left at an equal distance from two encampments. Competing gaucho teams lined up and galloped towards it, the aim being to get possession of the duck and carry it home. Whoever got the duck first was frantically pursued by the opposing team, whose members would do anything to seize the duck, including lassoing opponents with *boleadoras*, cutting saddles free and pulling men off their horses at full gallop. The game was considered so violent that in 1776 the Catholic Church threatened to excommunicate players.

Today *pato* has been toned down. Still, it's not exactly cricket. The hapless duck has long since been replaced by a large leather ball with six handles which is thrown, wrenched and passed between players on horseback who score goals by throwing it through a type of basketball hoop. The players may have swapped their sombreros and ponchos for American-style football helmets and leather kneepads but the spirit remains. If you're in luck you may be able to catch a *pato* game at an *estancia* or even at one of the *pato* tournaments in Buenos Aires.

Another popular gaucho game still played today is *sortija*, which is slightly reminiscent of a medieval jousting tournament. At full gallop and standing up in his stirrups, the mounted gaucho tries to aim a thin needle-like stick through a ring hanging from a pole. It requires incredible amounts of skill and superb horsemanship.

THEATRE AND CINEMA

When the dazzling Teatro Colón first opened its doors in 1908 with Verdi's *Aida*, a precedent was set for Argentina's arts scene. Designed by Italian architects with La Scala in mind, the lavishly decorated Colón takes up an entire block of central Buenos Aires. Inside, it is awash with red and gold trimmings, glittering chandeliers and exquisite sculptures, a grand reminder of Argentina's belle epoch. It is arguably the best opera house in Latin America and one of the greatest in the world. During the theatre season, which runs between April and December, an equally dazzling audience settle into plush velvet armchairs in the auditorium or stand shoulder-to-shoulder on the top-floor balconies.

The Teatro Colón is the jewel in what is a very glittering crown. Argentines love to go out to the theatre and cinema and will do so as often as possible. A few blocks away from the palatial Colón is Corrientes Avenue. Dubbed the 'street that never sleeps', it is choc-a-bloc with theatres. A *porteño* saying holds that you can go to the theatre every night for a month in Buenos Aires and see a different show each time.

Argentines are equal fans of the cinema and Argentine film has gained international renown. It has also been one of the few avenues in which the atrocities of the Dirty War are aired. Don't miss Luis Puenzo's *La Historia Oficial* (The Official Version), in which a middle-

Cinemas across the country have cheap days once a week, usually Wednesday, when ticket prices are slashed in half

class family comes to terms with the fact that its adopted daughter is the child of a disappeared victim kidnapped during the *Proceso*. It won an Oscar in 1986 for the best foreign film and attracted widespread international attention. Fernando Solanas' *Tangos, El Exilo de Gardel*, explores the lives of those living in exile in Paris during the military dictatorship. Maria Luisa Bemberg's *Camila*, set 150 years earlier during the dictatorship of Juan Manuel de Rosas, retells the true story of Camila O'Gorman, the daughter of a wealthy creole landowner who fell in love with a priest and was eventually executed. The parallels of Rosas' days portrayed in the film—torture, state terrorism, dissidents' disappearance and liquidation—with the recent military dictatorship weren't lost on anyone when the film was released in 1984.

Current cutting edge Argentine directors to keep an eye on include the neorealist Lucrecia Martel whose 2001 *La Ciénaga* tells the story of two large families trying to cope with each other during a long, sluggish summer in Salta. Her widely acclaimed film *La Niña Santa* (2004) explores the conflicts of sex and religion through the eyes of a teenage girl. Pablo Trapero's *El Bonaerense* (2002) tells the story of corruption and lives of Buenos Aires Province police officers while his 1999 film *Mundo Grua* portrays the life of a migrant worker. Works by the director Fabián Bielinsky, whose untimely death in 2006 was a great loss to Argentine cinema, include the fast-paced caper *Nueve Reinas* (2000) and the thriller *El Aura*(2005). Argentine films are received with obvious anticipation by local audiences, but Hollywood blockbusters are also wildly popular. Come prepared, though, for a confusing stream of jazzed up Spanish titles. For example, Kenneth Brannagh's production of Shakespeare's *Much Ado About Nothing* went under the title of *Much Noise, Few Nuts*, while The *Sound of Music* played under the racy title of *The Rebel Nun!* Appealing to the Argentine sense of mischief, many other movie titles are loaded with lots more sexual or romantic innuendoes than the original English title lets on. Meanwhile, bearing in mind the Argentine passion for late nights, it's not altogether uncommon to go to the cinema at two in the morning—look out for the *trasnoche* show.

MUSIC AND SONG CONTESTS

Argentines have an unbelievably high tolerance level for noise and generally there is always music blaring out from somewhere. Argentine rock is famous throughout Latin America, although it is still to take the foreign markets by storm. And even though I've never before been to a country with such an obsession with the Rolling Stones, Argentina has produced its own fair share of contemporary rock legends. Charly Garcia and Fito Paez effortlessly fill stadiums and sing songs that reflect the reality of Argentine life. They have a rebellious streak—Garcia's rendition of the Argentine national anthem once landed him in court.

At the other end of the spectrum are the folkloric singers Mercedes Sosa and the younger up-and-coming Soledad Pastorutti, who was a teenager when she released her first album. Both are hugely popular among Argentina's youth, proving that *folklorico* isn't just for fuddy-duddies. In fact, Sosa frequently appears with Garcia on stage.

You won't have to head to packed stadiums to hear Argentine music at its best. Spontaneous song contests (*payadas*) take place in crowded unpretentious bars. Competitors are often dressed in the full gaucho get-up—baggy *bombacha* trousers, sombrero, *rastra* and neck scarf, complete with a large curling *facón* stuck into their waistband. These men leap up and improvise verses, challenging the other *troubadours* in the room, who in turn sing a withering response between puffs on their cigarettes and swigs of red wine. Stumbling into a bar in the Buenos Aires suburb of Mataderos one late Sunday afternoon, we found an entire room entranced by these *payadores*, heads swivelling from one end to the other like spectators at a tennis match. All the time, the barman, who doubled up as the guitarist, never missed a beat or a chance to refill an empty glass. An especially good verse would be greeted with applause and bravos, begging a response. Anyone who could hold a tune and sing loudly enough was welcome to join in.

THE TANGO

Tango, of course, is not the only music and dance native to Argentina, but it is by far the most sensational. What's more, it is quintessentially Argentine and this is no mean feat in a country that complains it has few truly national inventions.

Funnily enough, in this most macho of countries, the tango began in a remarkably un-macho way. It was danced by pairs of men as they queued in brothels, to the music of the violin, guitar and flute. Later, the *bandoneón* was added. This musical instrument—a German invention that looks like a sort of elongated accordion with buttons instead of keys—provides the telltale melancholic wheeze that we associate with the tango today. As the flutes disappeared and a piano was added, the tango seemed to take on a desperately sad air and one that complemented the life of the lonely immigrants who arrived in Buenos Aires at the turn of the century. Enrique Santos Discépolo, a great tango composer, once defined the tango as a "sad thought that is danced." A slightly more optimistic observer called it "the happiness of being sad."

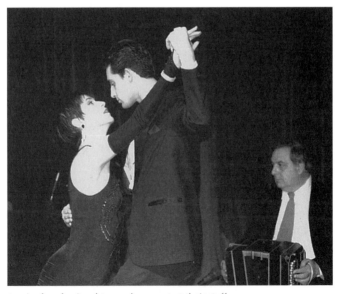

A pair of professional tango dancers strut their stuff.

Underneath its melancholic veneer, the tango can be surprisingly raunchy. "Dancing the tango is like having an affair that lasts for three minutes," said a friend who had been seduced by the tango when she arrived in Buenos Aires and avidly taking evening lessons ever since. I could see her point. When you watch a couple dancing the tango, lips a matter of millimetres away on the verge of a kiss and chests pressed close together, it's impossible to believe that they're not having a love affair in real life. The chances are, however, that they're not. In fact, they may never have even spoken to each other before.

A nod, a smile or a glance to the dance floor is enough for a man to invite a woman to dance the tango. He then walks over to her table and she stands up to meet him. No words are exchanged. Never, in Argentina, will a woman be so bold as to invite a man to dance the tango. This sounds terribly macho, but it is an unbreakable rule that is adhered to at all costs. Once on the floor, it is the man again who leads. He moves forward, she moves backward. The subtle pressure of his hand on her back lets her know a change of direction or when to perform a gliding figure of eight step known as an *ocho*. They also both need an inbuilt radar to avoid colliding with other couples on the dance floor—technically a big tango no-no.

Tango fashion has a distinct look that tells of its origins in city brothels. Fishnet stockings, high heels and clingy dresses are de rigueur for women, lacquered hair and neck-scarves for men. Preferred colours are red and black. Mind you, while some tango dancers look like they've just stepped out of a cabaret, with gloves up to their elbows and feathers in their hair, others may well appear in jeans and a T-shirt. Still, no female tango dancer worth her salt would even dream of dancing in anything lower that two-inch heels! In fact, tango lyrics frequently refer to clothes: "*Don't you remember that with me you wore your first hat and some leather belt that I stole/ Didn't I bring you, for your saint's day, a lovely pair of earrings that I nicked from that jerk's room one night/ As well as those suede boots and that great silk skirt …*"

A statue of Carlos Gardel.

But above all, tango touches upon matters of the heart, or rather the broken heart. The song that Argentines generally consider one of the greatest tangos ever released tells the story of a man, probably a pimp, complaining bitterly about the loss of his lover. *Mi Noche Triste* (My Sad Night) was the first tango sung in public by Carlos Gardel. This is a rough translation of Pascual Contursi's lyrics:

Woman, you left me during the most important period of my life

You are leaving me with a broken soul and thorns in my heart

You knew that I really loved you

And that you were the source of my joy and my torrid dreams

I am now without consolation and am getting drunk to help me forget.

The Magic of Gardel

Carlos Gardel was born in Toulouse, France in 1890, and taken to Buenos Aires at the age of three by his single mother. Some historians have suggested that he might have been Uruguayan, and there's even doubt that his real name was Gardel. But whatever his origins, there's no doubt that once Carlos Gardel opened his mouth he was 100 per cent *porteño*. It is his face with the perennial smile beneath the trilby that beams from photos in old cafés throughout the country.

In 1917, Gardel did what no *porteño* had ever done before; he sang a tango, *Mi Noche Triste,* in front of a genteel *porteño* audience at the Esmeralda Theatre in Buenos Aires. Tangos had been sung before, but only in bars and houses of disrepute. Now suddenly here was a man singing about a broken-hearted pimp that had decided to get drunk. What's more, he was singing in *lunfardo*, the local street slang of Buenos Aires. It was a tremendous hit.

Sadly, Carlos Gardel was killed in a plane crash in Colombia in 1935, cutting short a promising film career. Dozens of fans were so distraught that they tried to commit suicide. More than 60 years after his death, Argentines talk about Gardel as though he's still alive. A common Argentine saying claims that 'Gardel sings better every day'. If someone's singing is not up to scratch, a real put-down would be, 'He's no Gardel.' (Ouch!) And when Diego Maradona scored a third goal against Greece in the 1994 World Cup, a popular Argentine radio journalist, beside himself with excitement, whooped, "Gardel is alive! Gardel is alive!"

How to Become a Tanguero

There are two ways to enjoy tango in Argentina—as an observer and as an active participant. For the former, there is no end of venues where you can watch glitzy professionals perform electrifying tangos while enjoying a drink or an evening meal. And even if this seems slightly touristy, you won't be disappointed.

These polished shows probably aren't what you'd imagine tango to be all about. Where are the smoky bars, the glamorous clientele, the Carlos Gardels? For the real thing, you must go to a *milonga* (a tango hall). Here, for just a few pesos, you can walk in and drink, dance tango or just observe the absolute novelty of your surroundings. Every night, hundreds of true tango aficionados congregate in these *milongas*, silently and deftly gliding around the dance floor with the grace of 1930s movie stars. Old-timers, known as *tangueros*, dressed in neck-scarves and impeccable suits, invite high-heeled partners onto the floor, or sit round tables smoking and drinking red wine while eyeing up potential dance partners. You will feel you've walked into some sort of time warp.

At first sight this might look fairly intimidating, but don't let that put you off. A surprising number of younger Argentines are now taking up the tango too. Still, if you're a complete novice, you should go to a *milonga* that holds tango lessons earlier in the evening before a dance. That way, when someone nods in your direction, you can get up and not make a complete fool of yourself.

My first tango lesson was spent dancing lovingly with, well, a chair. But by lesson number two I had found a dance partner. His name was Nicolas, a 22-year-old graphic designer from Buenos Aires with extremely long hair and flared jeans. I was surprised. This was not the stereotypical *tanguero* I'd been expecting.

"It's all the rage among our age group now," he told me. "I guess it's fashionable in Europe so that makes it fashionable here."

"There's a tango revival going on in the whole world," Mario Sejas, the administrative director of Argentina's

National Tango Academy, told me. "Now it's beginning to capture the young as well. Old people like myself lived in a time when tango was the only music that we could listen to. This was lost by later generations and they stopped playing it altogether on the radio, but for the last few years it has been making a comeback. You can now hear it at more places and you can dance it in more places." Argentina now boasts a cable channel, Solo Tango, a radio station at 92.7 FM that belts out 24-hour non-stop tangos, and even three tango magazines, distributed free.

After just two classes, tango certainly got a grip on me and I was raring to go again.

'You see, that's the problem with tango,' Katya, an English friend living in Buenos Aires, confided. 'It's an addiction. First you go once a week, then twice a week, then before you know it you're going every night. I won't even leave the house without my tango shoes now.'

LA FIESTA

The melancholic strains of the tango are counteracted by the boisterous days of Carnival. Held over several days in February, Argentina's Carnival is neither as disorderly as Bolivia's nor as flamboyant and dressy as Brazil's, but it is a time when everyone gets to let their hair down and behave like giddy schoolboys. Two key ingredients put the oomph into Argentina's carnival: water bombs and cans of fake snow. You should know in advance that these will be chucked at you and sprayed on you at any given moment. Everyone is considered fair game. Other festivals—especially those in the northwest of the country—can be equally boisterous with packed plazas, gaucho parades and *asados* sizzling on every corner.

CALENDAR OF FESTIVALS AND HOLIDAYS

Practically every day in the year is claimed by some commemoration, be it Mother's Day, Lover's Day or just National Dog Day (June 2, if you were interested). Most of these don't amount to more than a fleeting mention in the newspapers and an excuse for a day off work for whoever's special day it is.

The dates that follow are only approximate guidelines, as they tend to change to suit long weekends, the weather, a last-minute whim or a case of *mañanaitis*. To get exact dates closer to the time as well as information on local fiestas, contact the government tourist office whose address is listed in the Resource Guide.

January

During the first 15 days, the Fiesta de Doma y Folklorico takes place in an amphitheatre in Jesus Maria, Córdoba. There is a 10-day event with singing, gaucho parades and a spectacular rodeo.

During the last week of January, the National Folkloric Festival is held in Cosquin, Córdoba.

February

Carnival celebrations throughout the country, lasting for two weeks. Particularly spectacular in the northern provinces.

March

During the first week of March, the Vendimia wine festival

Preparing for a gaucho parade in Salta.

is held in Mendoza. The central hub is in the open-air amphitheatre in Mendoza's Parque San Martín. Grapes are stamped by beauty queens, and there is music and dancing. Book early for accommodation.

March/April, Easter week celebrations throughout the country. National holidays on Maundy Thursday, Good Friday and Easter Day.

May
1, Labour Day, national holiday.
25, Anniversary of the 1810 revolution, national holiday.

June
10, Brits, keep a low profile: today is Malvinas Day, national holiday.
20, Flag Day (*Día de la Bandera*), another national holiday.
14–20, Salta Week, to commemorate the death of General Martín Guemes with parades, dances and bonfires in Salta.

July
9, Independence Day, national holiday.

August
15, Argentina's only bullfight—Toreo de la Vincha—to celebrate the Assumption of the Virgin takes place in Casabindo (Jujuy). The bull, which represents the devil, isn't killed; instead men try to remove ribbons and silver coins from its horns.
17, Anniversary of the death of General José de San Martín, national holiday.
23–24, Exodo Jujeño: week-long festivities in Jujuy to celebrate the city's evacuation under General Belgrano's orders in the early 19th century.

September
15, the city of Salta holds a religious festival when images of the Lord and Virgin are paraded through town to prevent earthquakes.

October

12, Columbus Day (Día de la Raza), national holiday.

Starting the second week of October and lasting 11 days is the Fiesta del Sol in San Juan city with folkloric shows, music and exhibitions.

First half of October, Oktoberfest beer festival in the Germanic town of Villa General Belgrano, Córdoba province.

November

1–2, All Souls Day or Day of the Dead celebrated by towns in the Quebrada de Humahuaca (Jujuy).

10, Día de la Tradicion. Gaucho festivals are held throughout the country with traditional parades, games, events on horseback, music and dancing. Excellent in San Antonio de Areco, Buenos Aires province.

Saturday in mid-November the Marcha del Orgullo Gay (Gay Pride March) takes place in downtown Buenos Aires.

December

8, Feast of the Immaculate Conception, a non-working optional holiday.

25, Christmas Day, national holiday.

LEARNING THE LANGUAGE

CHAPTER 8

'The first stirrings of man must have been dance
and the language of poetry. With these instruments,
man expresses his fears and hopes, he makes his
invocations and tries to communicate.'
—Jorge Luis Borges

At times, Argentines sound more Italian than Spanish. And like Italians and other Latin Americans their sentences are usually accompanied by flamboyant gesticulations and lots of touching. You won't have to adopt such characteristics, but your efforts at speaking Spanish will be enormously appreciated. In fact, you won't be able to fade into the background in a conversation with the Argentines, who are an incredibly chatty and expressive people. You'll be drawn into conversations whether popping into the corner shop, waiting in a bank queue or squeezed in a bus. Just make sure you raise your voice so you can be heard above everyone else's clamour.

If you haven't mastered Spanish before you arrive in Argentina, you may well be surprised at how fast you'll pick it up thanks to all the practice you'll get once you start mingling with Argentines. Children, especially, tend to find it ridiculously easy, probably putting you to shame in the process.

If you do find that you are stumped for the right words, you won't have much trouble finding someone who speaks English, especially in the major cities, larger hotels and within business circles. And even if you are fluent in Spanish, most Argentines just won't be able to resist practising their English on you anyway. Many Argentines also speak, or at least understand, Italian, Portuguese, French and German.

But undoubtedly the best advice is to try and learn a few Spanish basics before you actually arrive in Argentina. This is not as daunting as it may seem. As far as foreign languages go, you couldn't have picked an easier one. The Spanish language is remarkably straightforward and basically phonetic, with each letter consistently sounding like its name. A good pronunciation together with a foundation of vocabulary and grammar should mean that within a few weeks you'll be perfectly adept at ordering your *bife de chorizo* and holding your own in riotous conversation over *mate* with your new Argentine friends. Even the shyest students of Spanish shouldn't hesitate to practise their newly acquired skills—you will be adored for doing so.

PRONUNCIATION

With most consonants pronounced almost exactly as they are in English, vowels play a crucial role in successful listening and speaking. Each of the five vowels never vary in pronunciation.

A is pronounced AH, like the *a* in father.

E is pronounced EH, like the first *e* in elephant.

I is pronounced as a shortened and sharp EE, like the *i* in tangerine.

O is pronounced as a short OH, like the *o* in dot.

U is pronounced like a shortened OO, like the *oo* in oops!

Only two Spanish consonant sounds do not exist in English: the ***rr*** which sounds like a trill (the tongue must flutter) and the ***j***, as well as the ***g*** (when it comes before an e or an i), which sounds like someone clearing his throat, or like the *ch* in the Scottish *loch* or the German *ach*. A single *r* at the beginning of a word will also be rolled. Practise saying *que rapido ruedan las ruedas del ferrocarril*. If a native Spanish speaker can hear you say this without cringing, then you've probably mastered it.

There are some consonants that do not sound like their English counterparts:

H is silent.

Ñ is pronounced like the *ni* in onion.

QU is pronounced like the *k* in duck, with a silent *u*.

V is pronounced like a soft *b*. (To be clear with spellings, the Argentines will talk about *b larga* [tall *b*] or *v corta* [short *v*].)

Z is the same as *s*, with no buzzing or lisping sound as there is in Spain.

Most Argentines, but especially those from Buenos Aires, pronounce the ***y*** and ***ll*** like the softened *zsh* sound found in the English words *measure* and *beige*. Thus *calle*, meaning 'street', would be pronounced *caishay* and *yo* (I) would be pronounced *zshoh*. In some parts of Argentina and most of the Spanish-speaking world, both the *ll* and the *y* are pronounced like the English *y* in yes.

Stress

Generally, if a letter in a word has an accent on it, then that letter should be pronounced with greater stress. If a word has no accent and ends in a vowel, or in *n* or *s*, then the second to last vowel is stressed. For words ending in a consonant other than *n* or *s*, the last syllable is stressed.

VOSEO

In addition to the giveaway accent and incredible slang (see below), in everyday Argentine Spanish, a telltale characteristic that distinguishes Argentines (and Uruguayans) from the rest of the Spanish-speaking world is their use of the grammatical form known as the *voseo*. In this form, the second person singular, *tu*, informal, meaning 'you', is substituted by the more stylised word *vos*. When the *voseo* is used, verbs will be conjugated slightly differently than in regular Spanish, usually taking on an extra accent. It is a shady topic that can throw even advanced students of Spanish. For example, *tu* comes (you eat) becomes *vos comés* in Argentina. In irregular verbs the difference is more striking. *Tu entiendes* (you understand) becomes *vos entendés*, *tu eres* (you are) becomes that giveaway Argentine expression *vos sos*. With no obvious pattern, these irregular verbs must be learnt individually. If you do get hopelessly confused, you can always resort to the original *tu* form which everyone understands, but this will immediately identify you as an outsider.

Throughout the Spanish-speaking world, the formal version of both *vos* and *tu* is *usted*, but in Latin America (including Argentina), the second person plural of both *tu* and *vos* is *ustedes* and never *vosotros* as it is in Spain.

KEY WORDS AND PHRASES
The following key words and phrases should provide you with a handful of very basic Spanish starters.

Greetings and Initial Meetings

English	Spanish
Good morning	*Buenos días*
Good afternoon	*Buenas tardes*
Good evening/Goodnight	*Buenas noches*
Hello/hi	*Hola*
Pleased to meet you	*Encantado (encantada for a woman)/Mucho gusto*
How are you? (formal)	*Como esta usted?/Como le va?*
How's it going?/How are you? (informal)	*Como andas?/Como estas?*

English	Spanish
Very well, thanks, and you?	*Muy bien gracias, y vos/usted?*
Please	*Por favor*
Thank you	*Gracias*
Thank you very much	*Muchas gracias*
You're welcome	*De nada/no hay porqué*
Goodbye	*Ciao/Adios*
See you later	*Nos vemos*
See you tomorrow	*Hasta mañana*
See you soon	*Hasta pronto*
Yes	*Sí*
No	*No*
I'm sorry	*Lo siento*
Excuse me	*Disculpe/Perdón*
I don't speak Spanish	*No hablo castellano*
Do you speak English?	*Habla usted ingles?*
I don't understand	*No entiendo*
Could you speak slower please	*Podría hablar más despacio, por favor*
What is your name? (formal)	*Como se llama usted?*
What is your name? (informal)	*Como te llamas?/Cual es tu nombre?*
Who shall I say is calling?	*De parte de quién?*
My name is John	*Me llamo John*
This is Maria	*Te presento Maria*
Where are you from? (formal)	*De donde es?*
Where do you come from? (informal)	*De donde sos?*
What do you do?	*A qué se dedica?*
Do you like Argentina?	*Le gusta Argentina?*

English	Spanish
I love it	*Me encanta*
How do you say …?	*Como se dice …?*
How do you spell …?	*Como se escribe …?*
Don't bother me!	*No me molestes!*
Go away! (informal)	*Andate!*
Leave me alone, please	*Déjame en paz, por favor*

Shopping and Eating Out

English	Spanish
Could I see the menu, please	*Puedo ver la carta, por favor*
I want	*Quiero*
I would like	*Quisiera*
Do you have …? (formal)	*Tiene …*
Do you have …? (informal)	*Tenés …?*
We would like to order, please	*Queremos pedir, por favor*
Would you like anything to drink?	*Algo para tomar?*
Let's make a toast	*Un brindis*
Cheers!/Bless you (after a sneeze)	*Salud!*
Bon appetit!	*Buen provecho!*
breakfast	*desayuno*
lunch	*almuerzo*
supper	*cena*
dessert	*postre*
I'm vegetarian	*Soy vegetariano*
The bill, please	*La cuenta, por favor*
Where can I buy …?	*Dónde puedo comprar …?*
Where can I find …?	*Dónde puedo encontrar …?*
How much does it cost?	*Cuánto cuesta?*

English	Spanish
How much is it?	*Cuánto es?*
Do you have anything cheaper?	*Tiene algo más barato?*
Do you accept credit cards?	*Aceptan tarjetas de crédito?*
I'll take it	*Lo llevo*
Do you have this in my size?	*Tiene esto en mi talle?*
What size are you?	*Que talle es?*
I'm a 42	*Soy 42*
What shoe size do you take?	*Cuánto calzas?*
I take a 40 shoe size	*Calzo 40*
Give me a kilo of … please	*Deme un kilo de … por favor*
a pound	*una libra*
a litre	*un litro*
a metre	*un metro*

Directions and Travel

English	Spanish
Where is …?	*Dónde esta/queda …?*
How do I get to Córdoba?	*Como puede llegar a Córdoba?*
On the right/left	*a la derecha/izquerida*
straight on	*derecho*
up	*arriba*
down	*abajo*
one block	*una cuadra/manzana*
the bathroom/toilet	*el baño*
the tourist office	*la oficina de turismo*
the post office	*el correo*
the bank	*el banco*
the hospital	*la hospital*

English	Spanish
the embassy	*la embajada*
the main square	*la plaza principal*
the train station	*la estación de ferrocarril*
the bus stop	*la parada*
the airport	*el aeropuerto*
aeroplane	*avión*
bus terminal	*terminal de buses*
the bus	*el colectivo*
the subway	*el subte*
ticket	*boleto*
return ticket	*boleto ida y vuelta*
When does the next	*Cuando sale el próximo avión/*
plane/train/bus for … leave?	*tren/colectivo para …?*
Do you have a room?	*Tiene un cuarto?*
For one/for two	*para uno/para dos*
With a private bathroom	*con baño privado*
With air-conditioning/ heating	*con aire condicionado/ calefacción*
Is breakfast included?	*Esta incluido el desayuno?*

Telling the Time

English	Spanish
What time is it?	*Qué hora es?*
Could you tell me the time please?	*Podría decirme la hora por favor?*
It's eight o'clock	*Son las ocho*
It's eight forty-five (literally nine minus a quarter)	*Son las nueve menos cuarto*
It's five thirty	*Son las cinco y media*

English	Spanish
It's one o'clock	*Es la una*
In the morning	*por la mañana*
At night	*de la noche*
Today	*hoy*
Yesterday	*ayer*
Tomorrow	*mañana*
Early	*temprano*
Late	*tarde*

Numbers

English	Spanish
1	*uno*
2	*dos*
3	*tres*
4	*cuatro*
5	*cinco*
6	*seis*
7	*siete*
8	*ocho*
9	*nueve*
10	*diez*
11	*once*
12	*doce*
13	*trece*
14	*catorce*
15	*quince*
16	*dieciseis*
17	*diecisiete*
18	*dieciocho*
19	*diecinueve*
20	*veinte*

English	Spanish
21	*veintiuno*
22	*veintidos*
30	*treinta*
40	*cuarenta*
50	*cincuenta*
60	*sesenta*
70	*setenta*
80	*ochenta*
90	*noventa*
100	*cien*
200	*doscientos*
300	*trescientos*
1000	*mil*
1,000,000	*un millon*

Days of the Week

English	Spanish
Monday	*lunes*
Tuesday	*martes*
Wednesday	*miércoles*
Thursday	*jueves*
Friday	*viernes*
Saturday	*sábado*
Sunday	*domingo*

Months of the Year

English	Spanish
January	*enero*
February	*febrero*
March	*marzo*
April	*abril*

English	Spanish
May	*mayo*
June	*junio*
July	*julio*
August	*agosto*
September	*septiembre*
October	*octubre*
November	*noviembre*
December	*diciembre*

PUTTING YOUR FOOT IN YOUR MOUTH

If you learnt your Spanish in Spain or in another Latin American country, take care. Argentines have invented new words and twisted all sorts of other words around. The most obvious potential faux pas is the word *coger* which for most Spanish speakers means 'to take' as in 'to take a bus'. In Argentina, however, *coger* means 'to have sex with someone'. In Buenos Aires, one would never *coge un colectivo*.

It is also worth noting that *facturas* are not only a bunch of bills and invoices as they would be in other Spanish-speaking countries, but can also mean something altogether much more delicious—an assortment of pastries, usually stuffed with sticky *dulce de leche* caramel, that go down a treat with a café *cortado* at teatime.

Beware, also, of the following false friends that English-speaking Spanish students must contend with: *preservativos* are condoms and not jam. If you are *embarazada*, you are pregnant and not embarrassed, while *nafta* in Argentina means gasoline and not the trade agreement.

SLANG

The use of slang in everyday speech is so extensive and widespread that Argentina could at times almost boast its own language.

As waves of immigrants from around the globe poured into the port of Buenos Aires, they brought with them their own languages, and many of their words stuck and are still used today. Since most of the immigrants came from Italy and Spain, what emerged as the local slang is derived from a ferociously fast blend of Spanish and Italian—a colourful and unique fusion known as *lunfardo*. Unless you've grown up speaking both Italian and Spanish at home, *lunfardo* is up there on the incomprehensibility stakes with London's rhyming cockney slang.

You will hear *lunfardo* spoken throughout the country, but its epicentre is Buenos Aires, where it was born in the brothels and city tenements at the turn of the century. Just a quick skip across the pages of a *lunfardo* dictionary and it becomes crystal clear that this was once the language of crooks, drunks, brothel customers, thieves, the down-and-out and the brokenhearted. (*Lunfardo* comes into its own when used in the lyrics of the tango.)

If you think you're confused now, *lunfardo* gets even stranger. In its most warped extreme it switches the last syllable of the word with the first syllable. Thus café becomes *feca*, *mujer* becomes *jermu*, *vino* becomes *novi*, and the tango becomes the *gotan*.

Try and get your hands on a copy of José Gobello's *Nuevo Diccionario Lunfardo* if you can.

'Argentinianisms'

The following words are used in everyday Argentine speech, and probably won't mean anything to you if you learnt to speak Spanish outside Argentina. Many of the words are unadulterated *lunfardo* and some are straightforward slang evolved over the years. Argentines also use the normal Spanish equivalent. (Wherever possible, the corresponding Spanish word is given in italics within parentheses.)

'Argentinianism'	English Meaning
alucinante	amazing/incredible (*increíble*)
atacado	hassled/stressed (*estresado*)
bache	pothole in the road; you'll come across a lot of these

'Argentinianism'	English Meaning
bárbaro	cool, great, fantastic (*estupendo/ magnifico*)
birra	beer (*cerveza*)
bocha	a lot (*montón*)
boliche	nightclub/disco (club/*discoteca*)
bolita	a Bolivian, derogatory (*boliviano*)
boludez	a stupid thing (*tontería*)
boludo/a	(literally big-balled), means something like dickhead or asshole; affectionate or aggressive form of address, depending on tone of voice
bondi	bus (bus/autobus) also known as a *colectivo*
bostero	Boca Juniors football club fan
brazuca	a Brazilian (*brasileño*)
bronca	fury/anger—to be mad at something or someone (*rabia*)
buchón	sneak/gossipmonger (*soplón/ chismoso*)
buena onda	good vibes/cool
cana	prison or the police, literally a grey hair (*cárcel/policia*)
canchero	show-off, a cool guy who knows it
catrera	a bed, especially one for frolicking (*cama*)
chabón	man, guy or bloke (*hombre*)
chancho	ticket collector, derogatory (*guarda*)
chanta	slightly sleazy charmer, greaser, fraud, chancer
che	friend, mate, hey you (a common form of address)

'Argentinianism'	English Meaning
china	girl or woman, men may talk about *mi china* (my woman), especially popular in the countryside where it is an old-fashioned name for a gaucho's girl (*chica/mujer*)
chorro	thief (*ladrón*)
coco	head, literally a coconut (*cabeza*)
encurdelarse	to get drunk, inebriated (*emborracharse*)
farándula	Argentina's jet set of models, TV stars, actors and polo players
faso	cigarette, but more often a marijuana joint
fiaca	bone idle, lazy, lethargic; if you have fiaca, you can't be bothered to do anything (*pereza*)
fifi	fashion-conscious man, dandy
flash	something cool/great
forro	condom or scumbag, vulgar (*condón*)
gallego	a Spaniard, due to the fact that many Spanish immigrants came from Galicia (*español*)
gallina	River Plate football club fan
gardeliano	fan of tango singer Carlos Gardel
gauchada	a favour, a spontaneous act of generosity
gaucho	the original Argentine cowboy, now used to describe a ranch hand or man from the countryside

'Argentinianism'	English Meaning
guacho	literally a stray but used as an insult, like 'bastard' (not to be confused with gaucho)
guita	money, cash (*plata/dinero*)
joya	great/good (*bueno*)
laburante	worker (*trabajador*)
laburar	to work (*trabajar*); work itself is laburo (*trabajo*)
loco	bloke/guy (literally a mad one)
luco	a thousand pesos
macana	terrible, as in *Qué macana*! What a shame!
macanudo	great, fantastic person, a good sport (*buen tipo*)
mango	a peso; if something costs 5 mangos, it costs 5 pesos
masa	a great/cool thing
milicos	the military (*militares*)
mina	girl—in tango lyrics it describes a gangster's moll, now for all young women (*chica/mujer*)
morfar	to eat (*comer*)
nafta	petrol/gas (*gasolina*)
ñoqui	a potato pasta traditionally eaten on the 29th of each month; also a public employee who shows up only on pay day
pajuerano	country bumpkin, yokel
papa	a beautiful thing of top quality or use
papelón	embarrassing thing or situation (*cosa vergonzosa*)
paraguas	a Paraguayan, derogatory (*paraguayo*)

'Argentinianism'	English Meaning
pedo	drunk (literally a fart), as in *estoy en pedó*/*tenia un pedo*—I am drunk/I was so drunk (*borracho*). If you are *al pedo*, however, it means you're not doing anything (*a la deriva*).
Pelotas	balls, usually used in the sense of *no me rompes las pelotas*—don't break my balls!
pelotudo	same as *boludo*
pendejo	insult, meaning a fool, stupid (literally pubic hair)
pibe/a	guy, kid (*chico/chica*)
pingos	the horses (at a race)
piola	used to describe something that is cool or trendy or someone who is cunning and astute
porteño	inhabitant of Buenos Aires, 'from the port'
potro	a cute guy
pucho	cigarette (*cigarillo*)
re	a prefix that means 'really' or 'very', as in *re-frio esta*—it's really cold
seco	dry/without money
tacho	taxi; a taxi driver may be referred to as a *tachero* (taxi)
tano	an Italian (*italiano*)
telo	hotel with rooms rented out on an hourly basis, also known as an *albergue transitorio*
trasnochador	someone who stays up all night, commonly encountered in Argentina

'Argentinianism'	English Meaning
trucho	bogus, fake, something that is not what it appears to be (*falso*)
turco	a generalisation to describe a Muslim or a member of the Syrian community in Buenos Aires
quilombo	a mess or a brawl (*lío*)
viejos	parents (*padres*)
vivo	someone on the ball, quick to react to a given situation; a typical *porteño*

Common Gesticulations

- A hand, palm down, stroking the underside of your chin away from the body means either a dismissive 'I don't know' or 'I don't care'.
- An outstretched arm with hand, palm down, making a scratching motion means 'come here'.
- A hand held palm up, with fingertips bunched together jabbing up into the air, means 'what's up?' 'what's going on?' or 'what's your problem?' A flashier variation involving both hands making the gesture is generally employed in times of great exasperation.
- A hand holding an imaginary pen in the air making short squiggles is a wonderfully easy way of asking for the check/bill in a crowded restaurant or café. The movement is usually accompanied by mouthing the words, *La cuenta, por favor*.
- Slapping the back of one hand into the open palm of the other is a sign for money that could mean 'he earns a lot', 'it costs a lot' or 'pay up, buddy'.
- The index finger gently pulling down the outer corner of the eye warns 'watch out,' 'keep an eye out on that guy' or 'I know what you're up to'..

Useful Insults

A few useful insults up your sleeve will prove invaluable, especially if you decide to take to the road. Insults in Argentina range from quite light-hearted jests to the rather more offensive. In a nation where the family is considered sacred, a slur on the female members (both mothers and sisters) is especially damning. The most commonly used offensive expression is *hijo de puta*, the equivalent of 'you son of a bitch'. If that is too extreme, you can always fall back on punchy little words such as *pelado* (baldy) or *gordo* (fatty). Spoken in the right tone, they can be quite offensive, especially if followed by the *suffix de mierda* (literally 'shitty').

Another popular Argentine insult is *boludo*, literally 'big-balled'. Said sweetly, this form of address can be quite affectionate and is commonly used between friends. Said in an angry tone, however, it can suddenly become remarkably abusive.

BODY LANGUAGE

Like most other Latin Americans, Argentines are very touchy-feely during conversations and their concept of personal space is vastly diminished in relation to the North American or North European norm. Don't jump back or try to edge away when an Argentine is hovering a matter of millimetres from your nose. Just as you shouldn't flinch if they grab your arm to emphasise a particularly important point or decide to casually pick lint off your suit.

Argentine men gathered together may appear to be acting in a way that doesn't seem awfully macho to an outsider. They will happily stroll down the street with their arms round each other and embrace and kiss old friends affectionately. At football matches don't be surprised to see grown men hug and kiss each other or burst into tears.

As you learn to speak Argentine Spanish, you will soon discover that most sentences are usually backed up with an incredible amount of hand and arm movements. I have known quite reserved foreigners who, like most of us, normally speak keeping their hands and arms perfectly immobile. But as soon as they start to learn Argentine Spanish, they automatically start to use amazing gesticulations. Then, when they revert to speaking their native tongue again, they cease flapping their arms about. It happens to me all the time.

As difficult as it is to resist, don't be too eager to jump in with wild gesticulations until you have ascertained their true meaning. Certain gestures that are perfectly harmless where you come from could send out unintentional messages or even cause great offence in Argentina.

PIROPOS

As you walk along the streets of Argentina, don't be surprised to hear men murmuring suggestive comments to passing women. What you are hearing are known as *piropos* and such behaviour is considered perfectly normal.

In the good old days catcalls (or *piropos* as they are known here) always used to be snatches of poetry and romantic compliments. In modern times, *piropos* can still be lovely and eloquent gestures. However, occasionally they may also be slightly vulgar or involve inappropriate requests. Like chat-up lines in bars, women must ignore them and are never expected to respond or take the man up on his offer.

But *piropos* are not always that easy to ignore. As you (a woman) walk down the street, a man approaching from the opposite direction might well stop dead in his tracks, fling his arms wide open and blatantly eye you up and down. Then, once he's sure he's caught your attention, he will say something like "Darling, if beauty were a sin, then you'd be unforgivable!" or "My God, I didn't know that flowers could walk." I have seen grown women break out into giggles when this happens. Don't worry if you can't help but smile at the *piropo*; the man, needless to say, will be ecstatic. Of course, if a truly lovely compliment comes your way, a smile or a simple thank you is entirely acceptable.

HOT TOPICS TO TALK ABOUT

Argentines love to chat so don't worry about any awkward silences on your part; they will go unnoticed in the incessant background noise. You will soon discover that Argentines are quite capable of talking about anything for hours on end, ranging from mundane waffle to intense debates on the meaning of life.

Social customs in Argentina are all geared towards conversation. The whole art of the *asado* (barbecue) as well as the *mate* ritual provide the perfect excuse for a good chinwag. For this reason alone, you should never turn down an invitation to drink *mate* or eat beef.

If you do come unstuck, which is enormously unlikely, here are some key conversation pointers:

- Football: Given the country's obsession with football (soccer to North Americans), this is naturally a great starting point. Just make sure you know your Maradona from your Pele or you risk making a fool of yourself. Everyone in Argentina—young, old, male and female—has a fair grasp of the basics of the game just as everyone also has an opinion and a team that they back until death. To swap teams or allegiances is abominable, so don't suddenly become a Boca Juniors fan just because it seems everybody else is. I once observed a middle-aged German man from Frankfurt who couldn't speak a word of Spanish having the most animated conversation with a teenager from Salta who couldn't speak a word of German. Only a discussion on the World Cup would allow this. Learn some phrases such as *De que cuadro sos?* or *De que equipo sos?* (Which football team do you support?) and just see the glint light up in their eyes.

- Family: This is another great topic of interest in Argentina where everyone is considered fair game for probing inquiries into their private lives and marital status. Whether you are married, have children or are thinking about getting married are all standard questions that you'll be expected to answer on spec.

- Fashion: You can't go wrong on this subject. Argentines are incredibly fashion-conscious and will love to know about any of the latest fashions from your neck of the woods. If you want to see just how easy it is to break the ice, try saying something like 'What a lovely skirt. Where did you get it from?' (*Que linda pollera, donde la compraste?*)

- Politics and the Economy: Argentines, in general, tend to be very well informed on current political and economic affairs and enjoy discussing them in great detail. Many Argentines will be quite happy to tell you who they voted for in the last election, and why, and will have strong opinions on the day's news and issues.

  Discussions on politics and the economy can get quite heated, especially if you get onto the subjects of corruption, *peronismo* and the economic meltdown of 2001/2002. It's amazing how a common gripe can unite people. Complaining about queues, things that don't work, power cuts and broken elevators or even the lousy weather can also prove to be a real bonding experience.

  Argentines may frequently knock their own country, but don't be as enthusiastic on the subject yourself, at least with initial acquaintances. This also applies to the more sensitive subjects, such as the issue of ownership of disputed territories.

- Culture: Argentines love going out to cinemas and theatres, and make very demanding audiences, so this will provide endless material for discussions on the latest film or show. Because of their varied immigrant backgrounds and the fact that many Argentines themselves love to travel abroad, you will find yourself drawn into conversations on different cultures and countries around the world. In fact, just being foreign will give you an immediate advantage in the conversation stakes. Everyone will be desperate to know all about your home culture and how Argentina compares with it. Your positive comments about Argentina and its people will be hugely relished.

NAMES AND SURNAMES

When addressing people in Argentina it is worth noting that the Argentines generally tend to follow North American rules rather than the Latin American or Spanish norm for surnames. This makes things a lot more straightforward when addressing people formally or being addressed yourself as it involves just one surname. For example, if Maria Lopez marries Juan Sanchez, she will be known as Maria Sanchez. (In Mexico and other Latin countries, on the other hand, she would be known as Maria Lopez de Sanchez.) Meanwhile Juan and Maria's child—Juanito—will take just his father's surname: Juanito Sanchez. (The more traditional Latin American and Spanish custom combines both the father's surname with the mother's maiden surname, giving the child the name Juanito Sanchez Lopez.)

Argentines may well revert to the traditional Spanish custom of using two surnames on official documents, driving licences, passports and even in the phone book, especially if the surname is a common one and could be confused with others. Do remember, however, that this being Argentina, with its colourful multicultural background, there are bound to be exceptions to the rule. So remain fairly open-minded on the subject, and if in doubt play it safe with a simple *Señor* or *Señora*.

DOING BUSINESS

CHAPTER 9

'He had a lot of stocks and shares
And half a street in Buenos Aires
A bank in Rio, and a line
Of steamers to the Argentine ...'
—Hilaire Belloc, from the poem 'About John'
in the collection *Cautionary Verses*

THE BUSINESS ENVIRONMENT

Looking on the bright side, conducting business in Argentina combines the best of both worlds. Rather like its people, Argentine business involves a wonderful mix of European efficiency and Latin American flexibility. But this is no Latin backwater. The chances are that you'll find yourself dealing with very sophisticated businessmen and women, many of who hold MBAs from leading universities.

Argentines have a long and strong history of dealing with foreign business. With the economy slowly but steadily getting back on its feet after the 2001/2002 economic crisis, foreign investors are once again returning to the country. Foreign investment is actively encouraged by the government and investors now have the same rights and duties as nationals with few restrictions. Argentina is one of the four members of Mercosur, the Southern Cone Common Market established in 1991 with Brazil, Paraguay and Uruguay (while Chile, Peru and Bolivia are associate partners) which aims to eliminate internal tariffs and can boast a combined population of 226 million.

As a foreigner doing business in Argentina, you will be welcomed with open arms and treated with great friendliness. But don't get too blasé. You should also keep your eyes and ears open, and get everything down on paper and checked by a lawyer. "Do business as you would in New York or London," advises Joe Oppenheimer, a German-

Brazilian economist who has been working in Argentina since 1970. "The rules are the same."

IT'S NOT WHAT BUT WHO YOU KNOW

As in all Latin American countries, a tremendous amount of networking goes on in Argentina. If you need something done, someone you know will have a cousin who has a friend who is married to someone who can do what you want. It may be a convoluted path but it is often the most effective. Contacts are crucial, and if you plan to do business with or in Argentina make it a priority to develop as large a network of contacts as possible. To phone someone up and say 'I was given your name by so and so' will be a hundred times more effective than a cold call. This sort of name-dropping is rampant within the Argentine community; so don't think twice about joining in yourself. Any previous Argentine business partners, friends, even relations if you can dig some up, are ideal starting points. If you really are arriving completely cold, your local chamber of commerce or embassy should be able to point you in the right direction.

Once initial contacts have been made, make the time and effort to build lasting personal ties. These will always pay off in the end. You should never walk away from an Argentine associate on bad terms, even if you don't want to cut a deal. Argentine business is a very personalised world and if you leave on a bad note word might get around, closing doors to you later on.

You should also bear in mind that nepotism is perfectly acceptable in Argentina's business environment; in many cases, it is even expected. In some companies jobs and deals will be given to family members and close friends of the family first. This is especially the case in smaller companies, family-run businesses and in the government. In such cases, you can name-drop to your heart's content, but you will still come in second.

The economy started to climb out of the crisis in 2003 and agricultural exports soon hit a record high thanks to the cheaper peso and the growing demand of Asian markets.

FORGING BUSINESS RELATIONSHIPS

The better your relationship with your Argentine colleagues, the better your chances are of doing good business and reaching a deal. Luckily, Argentines are more than happy to be wooed. In the process of forging good relations, you will be required to put in a lot of preparatory hard work, tucking into long lunches and getting stuck in conversations on every subject except the business at hand. By the time you've wined and dined with your Argentine business associates, as is customary, you should be left with rewarding friendships as well as contracts. "It's like a courtship," says Oppenheimer. "You need a lot of subtlety. Try not to show that you want the deal that badly, you're going to have to beat about the bush a little."

It is also important to note that many Argentines often value the person with whom they do business more than the name of the company. If you change your negotiating team halfway through a deal, you may undermine previous good relations or even an entire contract.

Greetings and Meetings

Argentines are very warm and effusive. Friends and acquaintances greet each other with hugs and kisses. Even at a business meeting, unless it is very formal, introductions may be accompanied by kisses. Women kiss women, men kiss women, but men will shake hands with other men at the first meeting, especially in a business setting. If men know each other well, they may also kiss each other on the cheek. This may sound shockingly un-macho, but it is very telling of their Italian origins. Just across the border, in Chile or Brazil for example, men wouldn't dream of kissing each other hello.

It is unlikely that you'll plunge straight into the business at hand as soon as you walk through the door. After the effusive greetings, conversation will probably move on to social chitchat. Brush up on topics such as football, and be prepared to answer questions on your family, as these will almost certainly crop up. Keep the conversation light. Sensitive subjects such as the Dirty War, the Malvinas-Falkland Islands, relations with Chile, military dictatorships and government corruption can still touch a raw nerve and are best avoided in a business setting. Only when all the pleasantries have been dispensed with can you get down to business.

Once the meeting is over, don't run off straight away; it would be taken as an insult. Again, social niceties are called for. Allow things to run their natural course and wait until your Argentine hosts make the first move to leave.

The Art of Greasing Palms

Argentine law makes a difference between *propinas* (tips or incentive payments), which are legal and help speed things up that are going to be done anyway, and *coimas* (bribes), which are illegal. Someone who solicits a bribe is known as a *coimero* and is liable to criminal prosecution, as is the person who gives the bribe. Yet bribing is rife, and as one foreign businessman pointed out, "There are a lot of bribable people out there." *Coimeros* may

Argentina's economy is the third largest in Latin America and growing at a rate of about 8 per cent.

well seek you out, and in some cases this might make things run more smoothly. If confronted with such a situation, you should always use your own judgement but remember that bribery can be a bottomless pit. At best you might get away with having a reputation of being a 'sucker' who always 'pays up'; at worst you could wind up in jail.

Gift Giving

The question of whether or not to give presents is a grey area in business around the globe, and Argentina is no exception. Argentine companies have not arrived at the stage where gift giving is deemed inappropriate, but you still want to make it clear that your gift is just that, and not a bribe.

If your Argentine counterpart has young children you could bring a small gift for them—perhaps a football or rugby shirt from your home country. Gifts like these are always appreciated and can't possibly be misconstrued. Flowers are also welcome, especially if you are invited to the home of your business partners (in which case you should never arrive empty-handed). You could bring along a present that is connected with your business or your country's culture such as a glossy coffee-table book. Women, however, should exercise a little more caution when giving gifts to male colleagues in case it is misconstrued as a personal overture.

Christmas is a traditional—and suitable—time for gift giving in the Argentine business world.

LABOUR

Argentina has the most skilled and highly educated labour force in Latin America, with a workforce of over 15 million people. Unemployment, which rocketed above 20 per cent at the height of the economic crisis in 2002 has now fallen to 10 per cent but many Argentines find themselves working longer shifts for less pay and—if they can find the work—may hold down two jobs. There are also a vast number of labourers working the black market, who are paid 'cash in hand' for unskilled or low-skilled jobs. Estimates suggest that as many as 30 per cent of Argentina's workforce survive in this way. Their wages are low, their hours long and they receive no benefits. None of them pay any taxes either.

Many of these black-market labourers are from neighbouring countries and have entered Argentina illegally. Some denounce the exploitative labour conditions while others are desperate to keep their jobs. The immigrants often find themselves in the firing line accused of taking work away from Argentines. Yet many are willing to do the work that no one else wants to do for such little pay.

Workers' Rights and Conditions of Employment

The 48-hour workweek is standard in Argentina. Workers must have a minimum of 12 hours off between consecutive workdays and those in hazardous occupations are limited by law to a 6-hour day. Saturday afternoons and Sundays are obligatory rest days, although overtime is permitted and those employed in the service sector, particularly, tend to work over weekends. Children under the age of 14 are forbidden from working with certain exceptions for those employed in family-run businesses and in farming. A one and a half hour lunch break is standard in Argentina, although workers under the age of 18 and female employees are entitled to two-hour lunch breaks (with some exemptions).

The minimum wage is US$ 1 an hour or US$ 206 a month (most jobs pay substantially more) and a 13th month salary is compulsory, half of which must be paid at the end of June and the remainder at the end of the calendar year.

In 2005, the average annual salary in Buenos Aires city was US$ 23,500, although average salaries are usually about half this in the rest of the country. Top executives earn in the region of US$ 66,000.

Paid vacations range from 14 to 35 days a year in addition to the 11 national holidays listed in Chapter 7, but workers must be employed for at least six months to qualify. Employees who have worked for less than six months are entitled to one day's paid holiday for every 20 days of work, which works out much the same.

Medical benefits and pension schemes are in force in Argentina, with mandatory contributions of 23 per cent of a worker's wage from the employer and 17 per cent from the employee. Employers must also contribute 9 per cent of their employee's wages towards a family allowance payment for the worker and additional amounts for worker's compensation, unemployment, disability and insurance benefits. Fringe benefits such as subsidised meals, transport and housing are at the employer's discretion.

Trade Unions

Labour unions have traditionally been massive and centralised in Argentina. They peaked under Perón's government in the 1940s and 1950s when at one stage 50 per cent of workers belonged to unions. Trade union membership is now half that and although labour unions continue to be particularly strong in the metallurgical, automobile and banking industries and among state employees, they are losing some of their once formidable economic and political clout.

Union membership is voluntary and union members have their union dues deducted from their wages and forwarded to the union by their employer.

HIRING AND FIRING

Many jobs in Argentina begin with a three-month trial period—which can renewed up to three times—during which time the employer decides whether to take that person on permanently. During this time, which can rather unfairly last as long as nine months, the employee will receive few benefits (no paid vacation, no pension scheme). He or she can also be dismissed without any severance pay or advance notice of termination. Once this trial period is over, the employee is either hired or dropped. If hired, he or she then has full worker's rights.

Argentina has fairly strict laws on termination of employment. If an employee is fired with no reasonable cause then he or she is entitled to an advance notice of at least one month and severance pay at the rate of one month's salary for each year served with the company. If dismissal is a result of provable lack of work then the indemnity is cut by half. Such strict procedures have been criticised for hindering employment, as many employers are afraid to take on the added risks of compensation, preferring instead to use mandatory overtime or black-market labourers.

WOMEN IN THE WORKPLACE

Women in managerial positions are still such a rarity in Argentina that newspapers run articles on them. But with no more than 10 per cent of management positions being occupied by women, Argentina is still leagues ahead of most other Latin American nations in regard to equal opportunities. Meanwhile, a new generation of highly qualified female graduates is emerging, suggesting further change is on the way and that traditional macho prejudices are going to have to give way sooner or later.

Having said this, you are still dealing with a fairly macho society. Visiting businesswomen will be under as much pressure as their female Argentine counterparts to look glamorous and immaculately turned out. Should you walk down the street, let alone visit a factory, brace yourself for

The more successful your business, the prettier your secretaries. Argentine men can be maddeningly sexist at times.

piropos (suggestive comments) and sidelong glances from men. You are also bound to be asked about your marital status and whether or not you have any children. Such questions aren't meant to be personal intrusions, but rather highlight Argentines' genuine interest in and love of family life.

Although women form just a small percentage of Argentina's managerial scene, they still hold considerable clout at home. As a visiting businesswoman, you should be aware (and beware) of the possibility of jealous wives and girlfriends of your male Argentine business associates. They could easily cause business relations to collapse. It is not unheard of for female partners and employees to be dropped because of pressure back at home.

THE LANGUAGE BARRIER

Many Argentines speak English, especially those belonging to the business community, but any efforts at speaking

Spanish on your part will be very much appreciated.

Don't think you can go it alone, however, when it comes to marketing your product locally. If you imagine that translation will be the least of

Translated Documents

Business documents must be translated into Spanish by authorised public translators to have any legal standing in Argentina

your worries, think again. Everyone still giggles at the case of General Motors when it tried to market its Chevy Nova in Latin America. In Spanish, *nova* also means a type of star but said out loud it might just as well have been *no va*, which means 'it doesn't go'. Needless to say, sales rocketed after the name was changed.

But General Motors' faux pas was nothing compared to that of one US chicken chain which decided, when expanding into the Latin American market, to stick with its successful US slogan: 'It takes a tough man to make a tender chicken.' Unfortunately, in the translation, the slogan came across as 'It takes a man with a hard-on to make a chicken affectionate.' Argentines, I'm sure, would have found this hysterical. But I'm equally sure that no macho Argentine worth his salt would have eaten that chicken.

Language mix-ups such as these work both ways of course. One Argentine restaurant, in a bid to attract tourists, translated its menu into English. Unfortunately, it appeared to be offering 'revolting eggs' for breakfast and 'smashed potatoes' for lunch.

Translation and Interpreter Services

Good interpreters come at a price—about US$ 300 for half a day's work. There are cheaper options, but you generally get what you pay for. Even so, it is advisable to check costs before contracting an interpreter; some may count a short meeting as half a day's work and charge you accordingly. Your embassy should be able to provide you with a list of known interpreters and authorised translators. Hotels may also be able to help and it's always a good idea to check the classified section in the English language daily, the *Buenos Aires Herald*.

TIMEKEEPING AND OFFICE HOURS

If you are an obsessive timekeeper, you might as well bang your head against a brick wall. It may at times look like Europe, even talk like Europe, but Argentina is Latin America and runs on Latin time frames, unless of course English timing—*hora inglesa* or *hora americana*—is specified. Having said that, punctuality on your part for business meetings is important, even if your hosts don't show up on time themselves. You can gauge the importance of a particular meeting to your Argentine colleagues by their punctuality: a very important meeting will probably start on time. Argentines accustomed to doing international business are generally much more punctual than the rest of the country.

In Argentina, the *mañana* syndrome, or procrastination, isn't as bad as it is in many other Latin American countries, but it does exist to a certain degree. If someone tries to brush you off until tomorrow (*mañana*), get tough. Let them know you're only in the country for a few days (even if this is not strictly true) and that you have to be seen today or else. Still, you should expect things to take longer in Argentina and thus budget your time accordingly. You should also be prepared to invest considerable time in forging successful business relations. The worst thing you could do is come to Argentina with an attitude of 'let's get this over and done with as soon as possible'. Not only would such an approach be considered inappropriate business etiquette, it is also completely impractical in Argentina.

Generally, business hours begin between 8 am and 10 am and end between 5:30 pm and 7 pm, Monday through Friday. Top executives tend to arrive after their secretaries, at around 10 am and stay on later in the evening.

Government offices are open from 12:30 pm to 7:30 pm in winter, and from 7:30 am to 1 pm in summer. Banks are generally open between 10 am and 3 pm Monday to Friday. (Note: Banks are closed on all the national holidays listed in Chapter 4, and also on 30 December and on Bank Employee Day, 6 November.)

In the countryside, the institution of the siesta is alive and well, and many businesses may close between 2 pm and 5 pm. But as business becomes more international this custom, sadly, is becoming less acceptable. In Buenos Aires, where a siesta would probably do everyone some good, it is now practically unheard of. Even the traditional long lunches accompanied by a bottle or two of wine are no longer everyday occurrences. Lunch may be just a sandwich grabbed between meetings.

> The 24-hour clock is widely used in Argentina. This is probably due to the fact that 1 o'clock in the morning is often just as rocking as 1 o'clock in the afternoon.

The Argentines are night owls at heart so don't be horrified if your Argentine counterpart decides to schedule a meeting as late as 8 pm. Breakfast meetings, on the other hand, are practically unheard of, not least owing to the fact that breakfast is not considered a serious event in Argentina; typical early morning traffic chaos is another obstacle. If you are calling the shots or running on a tight schedule, you might, however, be able to get away with insisting on a business breakfast, but lunch is undoubtedly the best bet if you want to do business over the dining table.

Finally, don't even think about trying to do business during the holiday season. Offices are deserted during January and February (summer holidays) and for the middle two weeks of July (winter vacation). If there has been a good snowfall in the Andes, you shouldn't be surprised if your Argentine colleagues nip off at the last minute for a few days' skiing as well.

BUSINESS ATTIRE

Argentines can be terribly fashion-conscious and are bound to judge you, at least initially, on your appearance. Think more 'London—subtle and understated—than anything too flowery or straight off the latest catwalks of Europe. Conservative dark suits for both sexes really can't go wrong, "Although a great Italian suit," a foreign businessman confided, "will work wonders in Buenos Aires."

During the summer months (December to March) businessmen usually wear lightweight suits and business-women wear lightweight cotton or linen dresses and trousers. In winter (June to August) woollen clothing, overcoats and an umbrella will be necessary.

If business extends to evening entertainment, you may be expected to change into something dressier. Gala nights at the opera or ballet usually mean black tie or evening dress. Also be prepared for the fact that some restaurants, clubs and casinos have a strict dress code.

More Business Tips

- When dealing with numbers, full stops punctuate thousands and commas indicate decimal points.
- Don't schedule back-to-back meetings, as you could run into the most awful domino effect and end up being late for everything.
- Give a firm handshake; this is a sign of both strength (machismo at work again) and sincerity (you can trust me).
- Argentines tend to communicate in close proximity. Don't back away.
- A large quantity of business cards to distribute will prove invaluable and help clarify your status.
- Try not to get flustered about smoking. It's still a perfectly acceptable custom in Argentina where nearly every man and his dog puffs away. If you do light up, it is polite to offer your cigarettes around to others in the room.
- Just as you may have called upon a contact, you will be expected to reciprocate and use your own contacts to help out when called upon yourself.
- Try to get people's direct telephone numbers, or your call may get lost in a maze of secretaries, departments and awful electronic music.
- If you're not sure what to wear, err on the side of formality. A book should not be judged by its cover, but—initially at least—you will be.
- Any invitations, business or social, made in a social context should be reconfirmed later. Argentines aim to please and may accept an invitation that they have no intention of keeping.

'Latins are tenderly enthusiastic. In Brazil they throw flowers
at you. In Argentina they throw themselves.'
—Marlene Dietrich

Official Name
Republica Argentina

Capital
Buenos Aires

Flag
Three equal horizontal stripes of light blue, white and light blue; in the middle of the white stripe is a brilliant golden sun with a human face known as the Sun of May

National Anthem
Himno Nacional Argentino

Time
Three hours behind Greenwich Mean Time

Telephone Country Code
+ 54

Land
Argentina is located in Southern South America, bordering the South Atlantic Ocean between Chile and Uruguay; and with further land borders in the North with Bolivia and Paraguay; and with Brazil in the Northeast. The rich plains of the Pampas fan out from Buenos Aires; to the south lies

the flat rolling plateau of Patagonia; the rugged Andes run along the western border.

Area
2,766,890 sq km (106,802 sq miles)

Highest Point
Cerro Aconcagua (6,960 m/22,835 feet)

Climate
Mostly temperate, arid in northwest, subantarctic in southwest

Natural Resources
Petroleum, uranium, lead, zinc, tin, copper, iron ore, manganese and the fertile plains of the pampas

Population
40,060,000 (2006 estimate)

Ethnic Groups
White 97 per cent (mostly of Spanish and Italian descent); the remaining 3 per cent are *mestizo* (mixed white and Amerindian ancestry), Amerindian or other non-white groups.

Religion
Nominally Roman Catholic (92 per cent), Protestant (2 per cent), Jewish (2 per cent), other (4 per cent)

Official Language
Spanish

Government Structure
Argentina has a federal system of government along the lines of the United States. There are three branches of authority: the executive, headed by the president; the judiciary, headed by the Supreme Court of nine judges; and the legislative, which consists of a bicameral national Congress of 257 directly elected congressmen, each serving a four-year term,

and 72 senators (three per province, three from the Federal Capital) who each serve a six-year term. The president and vice-president are directly elected for a four-year term and are eligible for a second term.

Administrative Divisions
1 autonomous city (Buenos Aires Capital Federal) and 23 provinces (Buenos Aires, Catamarca, Chaco, Chubut, Córdoba, Corrientes, Entre Ríos, Formosa, Jujuy, La Pampa, La Rioja, Mendoza, Misiones, Neuquén, Río Negro, Salta, San Juan, San Luis, Santa Cruz, Santa Fe, Santiago del Estero, Tierra del Fuego, Antartida e Islas del Atlantico Sur and Tucumán,

Currency
1 Argentine Peso (Arg$) = 100 centavos

Gross Domestic Product
US$ 548.754 billion (2006 estimate)

Agricultural Products
soybeans, sunflower seeds, lemons, grapes, corn, tobacco, tea, peanuts, wheat, livestock.

Industries
food processing, motor vehicles, consumer durables, textiles, chemicals and petrochemicals, printing, metallurgy, steel.

Exports
edible oils, fuels and energy, cereals, feed, motor vehicles

Imports
machinery and equipment, motor vehicles, chemicals, metal manufactures, plastic.

Airports
1,381 (154 paved). Ministro Pistarini International Airport (more commonly known as Ezeiza) just south of Buenos Aires is the country's main airport.

FAMOUS ARGENTINES

Following is a guide to some of Argentina's famous and infamous sons and daughters (Key historical figures are dealt with in Chapter 2.)

Raúl Alfonsín

President from 1983 to 1989 and the first democratically elected leader since the return to democracy. Alfonsín, from the Radical Party, put many top-ranking military leaders in jail and set up a commission to investigate the disappearances under *El Proceso*. However, his administration was plagued with economic problems and hyperinflation, and he resigned several months before the end of his term.

Jorge Luis Borges (1899–1986)

Argentina's greatest literary hero, novelist, poet and essayist, whose works include *Labyrinths*, *Fictions*, *The Aleph* and *Dr Brodie's Report*. A classic Anglo-Argentine, Borges was brought up in 'a garden, behind speared railings and in a library of limitless English books' and had the speech and manners of an Edwardian gentleman. A virulent anti-*peronista*, Perón 'promoted' him from chief librarian to inspector of poultry. In later life he was blind. He died, aged 87, in Geneva where he is buried.

Julio Cortázar (1914–1984)

Arguably Argentina's most famous and most prolific 20th century novelist, whose books include *Los Premios*, *Rayuela* (Hopscotch), and *Queremos tanto a Glenda*. He wrote many of his novels in exile and was greatly influenced by James Joyce.

Juan Manuel Fangio

Formula One car racer, five times champion in the 1950s and arguably one of Argentina's best sportsmen. Fangio led a scandal-free life, kept a low profile and was a true gentleman. He died in 1995 and remains an idol.

Martín Fierro

Argentina's most famous (fictional) gaucho created by José Hernández in his epic poem of the same name. Practically every Argentine possesses a well-thumbed copy of this classic.

Leopoldo Galtieri

General who invaded Falkland Islands and head of the military junta from December 1981 to June 1982, Disgraced and dismissed as a drunk, he was imprisoned for five years before being pardoned by Menem under the amnesty laws of 1990. He died in 2003 while under house arrest for his role in *El Proceso*.

Charly Garcia

Eccentric grizzled rock hero with a trademark black-and-white moustache whose gravely voice still drives audiences wild. Thoroughly anti-establishment youth hero.

Carlos Gardel

Undoubtedly the greatest tango singer of all time, as well as an aspiring actor and a national hero. Never seen without his trilby and heart-stopping smile. When he died in 1935 in a plane crash many Argentines felt orphaned. His well-visited tomb in Chacarita cemetery is covered with plaques and flowers and a larger-than-life-size statue of 'the songbird of Buenos Aires'.

Susana Giménez

Impossibly chiselled TV diva and chat show hostess, with metres of platinum blonde hair and Zsa Zsa Gabor's eyes. She is widely adored throughout the country and her show *Hola Susana* gets huge ratings.

Ernesto 'Che' Guevara

Sexy 60s revolutionary who wore combat trousers and a beret and smoked cigars. Guevara was born in Rosario in 1928 and grew up in Córdoba where he studied medicine at the university. He became Castro's right hand in the Cuban revolution before being shot dead at the age of 39 in the Bolivian mountains trying to foment worldwide revolution. Still a big icon among Argentine students.

Néstor Kirchner

The Patagonian born politician, and former governor of Santa Cruz province, Kirchner was elected to the presidency in 2003. A centre-left *peronist*, he has been critical of Menem's neoliberal reforms. He was imprisoned during *El Proceso* and since coming to power has revoked the amnesty laws in which perpetrators of the Dirty War were immune from prosecution. It is widely anticipated that he will re-run for the leadership in the 2007 presidential election.

Mafalda

Cheeky comic cartoon heroine who is always asking questions and spouting her views on humanity. Mafalda, who loves the Beatles and hates soup, was created by the comic genius Quino in 1964 and has become both a top Argentine personality and something of a national heroine.

Diego Maradona

The *enfant terrible* and national hero of Argentina's football scene, Maradona grew up in Villa Fiorito, a shantytown on the outskirts of Buenos Aires. By the age of 15, he was playing in premier division matches for Argentinos Juniors. He later played for Boca Juniors, Barcelona and Napoli FCs. His greatest moment came in the 1986 World Cup in Mexico —where he earned the title of the most talented footballer the world had ever seen. He is now a popular TV presenter.

Carlos Saul Menem

President from 1989 to 1999, the flamboyant former governor of La Rioja was once described as the president who doesn't give a damn if Argentines laugh at him. The entire nation was gripped by his very public divorce—at one stage he had his wife evicted from the presidential residence after a tiff. He has since remarried a Chilean beauty (and former Miss Universe) 35 years his junior. Despite being a Peronist, once in office he opened up the market economy and introduced a wide-sweeping privatisation plan. His presidency has since been criticized for being corrupt and frivolous.

Carlos Monzón

Heavyweight boxing champion whose life was struck by tragedy. Monzón murdered his wife and died in a car crash shortly after being paroled from prison.

Fito Paez

Rock soloist from Rosario whose albums include *Tercer Mundo*, *El Amor Despues el Amor* and *Circo Beat*. Even the uninitiated listener will be drawn to his unique style.

Patoruzú

A much-loved cartoon character created by Dante Quinterno, Patoruzú first appeared in a comic strip in the 1930s and has been charming generations of Argentines ever since. Modelled on a Patagonian Indian with superhuman powers and a heart of gold, he is never seen without Pampero, his beloved horse, or Isodoro, his *porteño* (and *vivo*) sidekick.

Juan Domingo Perón

Undoubtedly the biggest name in Argentine politics, Perón rose to power on the back of a military coup in 1943 and was elected to the presidency three times. Despite his death in 1974, *peronismo* has remained a driving force in Argentine politics.

Eva 'Evita' Perón

General Perón's glamorous mistress and, later, wife. Evita is one of the most loved—and reviled—figures of Argentina's 20th century. She died of cancer in 1952, at the age of 33 and many Argentines still consider her a saint.

Astor Piazzolla

Tango musician and composer born in Argentina to Italian parents. Piazzolla spent much of his childhood in New York and is widely credited (and occasionally attacked) for bringing tango into modern times with jazz and classical fusions. He died in 1992.

Mercedes Sosa

Folkloric singer and much-loved motherly figure with an incredibly powerful voice, she performs tear-jerking renditions of South American classics.

Marcelo Tinelli

TV star and for the last decade Argentina's most popular entertainer. He is the handsome and funny host of *Showmatch*.

Jorge Rafael Videla

Protagonist of the 1976 coup and first leader of the military junta. He was succeeded by General Roberto Viola in 1981, who in turn was replaced by Galtieri. Videla and other military officers were imprisoned in 1983 but pardoned by Menem. He is now under house arrest on charges of kidnapping during *El Proceso*.

Virgin of Luján

Argentina's beloved patron saint is also more affectionately known as la Virgencita. Legend has it that in 1630 a wagon with a painting of the Virgin en route from Brazil wouldn't move until the painting was removed. And there it stayed at what is now the town of Luján. The Virgin is now housed in Luján's basilica and visited by 4 million pilgrims a year. It is said that she has appeared in visions on numerous occasions to many Argentines.

ARGENTINA'S CITIES AND OUTSTANDING FEATURES

The following key cities and features are listed in order of their distance by road from Buenos Aires city. So you can judge just how far away—or how close—you want to get from the Capital Federal. Population indicators are given: ***million plus, **half million plus, *100,000 plus.

Buenos Aires***

Argentina's capital of 13 million inhabitants is home to the tango, Boca Juniors football club and the best steak houses on the planet. All cities have their own tempo, but the difference is that Buenos Aires' races at about 161 km/h (100 miles/h). It is a huge, pumping, vibrating, living and breathing metropolis, the proverbial city that never sleeps. And if you like to party, it is heaven.

La Plata**

(64 km/40 miles southeast of BA)

The capital of Buenos Aires province, La Plata is renowned for its spectacular natural history museum, university and lots of grandiose public buildings. Designed with Washington, DC in mind, the city was built practically from scratch in 1882. There are no street names, only numbers.

Luján

(65 km/40.5 miles west of BA)

Dubbed the 'Holy City', Luján welcomes 4 million pilgrims a year, who come to pay homage to Argentina's patron saint, the Virgin of Luján. A statue of the Virgin is kept in Luján's neo-Gothic basilica, whose twin towers rise above the small town in a lovely riverside setting.

Rosario***

(295 km/183 miles northeast of BA)

Affectionately nicknamed the Chicago of Argentina, Rosario is the third largest city in the country, thanks to its strategic location and bustling port on the Río Paraná. Che Guevara was born here as well as many of Argentina's great rock musicians. You'll soon have to choose which side to support in the ferocious football scene between Newells Old Boys and Rosario Central.

Mar del Plata**

(418 km/260 miles southeast of BA)

More of a beach town than a city, Mar del Plata is the centre for the sea fishing industry. It also claims the biggest casino in the world (come dressed to kill). In the summer months of January and February the city's ranks swell from 500,000 to 3 million with the massive migration of sun-seeking porteños. If you can find any room on the beach, this is the place to be seen in summer. (Although the serious money swans off to Punta del Este in Uruguay.)

Paraná
(507 km/315 miles north of BA)
The capital of Entre Ríos province is close to large forestry, citrus plantations and cattle ranches. It sits on the eastern bank of the Río Paraná, just 27 km (16.8 miles) from the city of Santa Fé. The two cities are connected by the Hernandarias tunnel, which runs beneath the river.

Bahia Blanca*
(637 km/396 miles southwest of BA)
An industrial centre and well-run port with a natural harbour, the city was originally built as a fort against marauding Indians. Agriculture and petrochemicals are the mainstay of this city, which is set to become a major terminal for exports of liquid petroleum. It is also an important naval base.

Córdoba***
(701 km/435.6 miles northwest of BA)
Argentina's attractive second largest city is an important industrial centre with a strong history of militancy. The people are warm and friendly, speak in singsong accents and are slightly more down to earth than in Buenos Aires. Córdoba has wonderful colonial buildings, including a magnificent cathedral that dates from the 17th century. It swarms with young medics studying at Argentina's oldest university. It is also the gateway to the sierras of Córdoba, rolling hills and lakes that bring to mind the Swiss Alps in summer.

Corrientes* and Resistencia*
(936 km/581 miles and 1,008 km/626 miles north of BA)
These sister cities lie on opposite banks of the fast-flowing Río Paraná. Resistencia, the capital of Chaco province, is the

quieter of the two. Graham Greene chose Corrientes province with its appropriate backdrop of red earth and tropical palm trees as the setting for a kidnapping in *The Honorary Consul*. This area is the hub of northeast Argentina's agricultural industry. There's great carnival and great fishing. Keep an eye out for the aggressive dorado and the enormous surubi catfish, which can weigh as much as a large man—or better still, catch one yourself in the corrientino's classic weekend getaway at Paso de la Patria.

Mendoza**
(1,044 km/648.7 miles west of BA)
The wine capital of Argentina, Mendoza is surrounded by vineyards at the foot of the Andes. Huge plazas and wide, sweeping avenues make this one of the loveliest cities in Argentina, which can also boast 350 days of sunshine a year. It has a big-city feel and is modern and well laid out, but life seems slower here. Don't miss the wine festival held in the first week of March.

San Juan*
(1,106 km/687 miles northwest of BA)
Old-fashioned sun worshippers will simply adore San Juan which averages 9 hours of sun a day and only 100 mm of rainfall a year. Unfortunately it was also built on a fault line and most of the city was flattened by a massive earthquake in 1944. San Juan is now blessed with relatively few skyscrapers and beautiful tree-lined avenues. It is surrounded by vineyards and has a complicated but breathtaking system of dams.

La Rioja*
(1,159 km/720 miles northwest of BA)
Founded in 1591, much of La Rioja's colonial architecture survived an earthquake in 1894. La Rioja is small, quiet and provincial with the Sierra de Velasco hills as a backdrop. It is known as the city of orange trees and is also a big wine producer. There are hot springs, canyons and dramatic rock formations nearby.

Tucumán**
(1,202 km/747 miles northwest of BA)
San Miguel de Tucumán (its full name) is the city where history was made in 1816 when independence from Spain was formally declared. Glimpses of its former grandeur are seen in a massive park filled with monuments and statues of the heroes of independence and a beautiful colonial plaza in the centre. It is otherwise slightly shabby but friendly. Nearby are the Indian ruins of the fortified city at Quilmes, well worth a visit, although it is unbearably hot in summer.

The Iguazú Falls
(1,285 km/798 miles north of BA)
When Eleanor Roosevelt laid eyes on the Iguazú Falls rumour has it that she just shook her head and said, "Poor Niagara!" You can walk a few inches above the falls on a hair-raising system of catwalks. Don't look down at their corroded concrete foundations but keep your eyes open for the fabulous butterflies and bird life, including toucans, in this dramatic jungle setting. Terrifying boat trips take you up to the falls themselves, where no less than 5,000 cu metres (6,540 cu yards) of water per second plunge over a 70-metre (229 feet) drop.

Península Valdés
(1,291 km/802 miles south of BA)
There is a national park here, near the port city of Puerto Madryn on the windswept Atlantic coast. Take a boat trip to see whales, orcas, sea lions, elephant seals and penguins. In summer, Puerto Madryn fills up with Argentines who come for the beaches, wildlife and good scuba diving. In winter the area takes on a deserted air and even the penguins leave.

Gaimán
(1,340 km/832.6 miles southwest of BA)
Famous for its Welsh immigrants who arrived in 1865, Gaimán is probably the best-known Welsh village in the region, largely thanks to its splendid teahouses. Much of the local population still have Welsh names like Jones and

Edwards and even speak a little Welsh. Gaimán even holds an annual eisteddfod. Welsh chapels and delightful cottages overgrown with roses make this a green and pleasant, if not a little peculiar, oasis in the flat Patagonian landscape.

Cafayate

(1,380 km/857.5 miles northwest of BA)

This classic whitewashed *pueblo* is enchanting and it's easy to understand why it is so popular with tourists from all across Argentina. The whole town is hemmed in by rows and rows of vineyards. The Calchaquie valleys are nearby with small attractive colonial towns such as Cachi and Molinos.

Salta*

(1,508 km/937 miles northwest of BA)

This colonial city with a beautiful plaza surrounded by outdoor cafés, whitewashed balustraded buildings and spring like temperatures all year round is a popular holiday destination. You get spectacular views from the San Bernardo mountain, accessible by stone stairs or cable car. Salta is also home to the *empanada*—these cheese or meat patties are sold on every street corner. There are also good gaucho festivals.

Jujuy*

(1,536 km/954.4 miles northwest of BA)

Pronounced 'Hoo Hooey', the city's full name is San Salvador de Jujuy and it is the capital of one of Argentina's poorest and more isolated provinces. Relics of former colonial glory compete with dilapidated ruins, post-earthquake architecture and divine orange trees. A chaotic black market opposite the bus station peddles everything from coca leaves to flip-flops. Nearby is the Humahuaca valley with its spectacular arid landscapes and famous folkloric festivals.

Bariloche

(1,597 km/992 miles southwest of BA)

Bariloche is reminiscent of a Swiss ski resort with its chocolate-box scenery of woods and mountains on the shore of the 96 km (60 mile) long Lake Nahuel Huapí. It enjoys fierce rivalry with Las Leñas for skiing, but Bariloche wins hands-down for its buzzing social life. The town itself has a year-round holiday atmosphere and is packed with clubs and discos that charge a small fortune at the door.

Comodoro Rivadavia*
(1,711 km/1063 miles south of BA)
The centre of Argentina's petroleum industry, Comodoro Rivadavia is the largest city in Patagonia's Chubut province. It is a modern coastal town (no plazas here) whose rise has been tied to the oil industry. To the south are beach resorts where you can observe sea lions—the water may be too icy for a swim yourself. Further afield are the *Cuevas de las Manos*, prehistoric caves with 10,000-year-old images of hands, guanacos and other animals stencilled on the walls.

Río Gallegos
(2,484 km/1543.5 miles south of BA)
There isn't much to see in the city itself, but as the capital of Santa Cruz province, it is strategically placed at the end of the world, a human oasis in a land of sweeping Patagonian plains, enormous skies and rough seas, where sheep outnumber men 50 to one.

El Calafate
(2,732 km/1796.6 miles southwest of BA)
El Calafate is criticised in guidebooks for being touristy with inflated prices, but its location on the southern shore of Lake Argentino is so beautiful that many *porteños* have decided to up sticks and live there permanently (and make a killing off the gringos). The town's population doubles during the summer months as El Calafate is the last port of call for all those going to Los Glaciares National Park.

Los Glaciares National Park
Argentina's second largest national park (600,000 hectares/ 1,482,600 acres) borders Chile and is home to the Fitzroy mountain range and the famous advancing Moreno glacier, where the occasional tourist used to be killed every season

by flying ice. This is the world's third largest ice field (after Antarctica and Greenland) and the lakes and rivers fed by the glaciers have the amazing colours of mineral-rich waters. Scenery freaks will be in heaven. Not to be missed!

Ushuaia

(3,070 km/1907.6 miles south of BA)

Set in a stunning location on the shores of the Beagle Channel in Tierra del Fuego and surrounded by the snow-capped Martial Mountains, Ushuaia captivates. Maybe it's the way the weather constantly changes from snowy blizzards to bright winter sunshine, but the world's southernmost city is also a tax haven and filled with ski centres, a buzzing nightlife and cute huskies from Antarctica. And if you don't like the weather, say the locals, just wait five minutes.

CULTURE QUIZ

And now for a chance to put your newly acquired skills to the test …

SITUATION 1

You are invited to drink *yerba mate* with some Argentine friends but you've still got to get used to the withered bitter taste that reminds you of boiled straw. Everyone else is partaking like good gauchos. Do you:

A Join in?
B Decline with a polite *gracias*?
C Tell them 'No way!' and ask incredulously how on earth an entire nation can be hooked on something so vile?

Comments

An offer of *mate* is a gesture of friendship and a sign of acceptance and therefore should never be rejected, so **A** is always the best response. If you persevere you might actually start enjoying it. If you really can't stomach the brew, then answer **B**. Your Argentine friends will understand you're just being a gringo with bad taste. Never answer **C**. Argentines adore their *mate*. This is not just any old drink, it's a lifestyle and an essential part of Argentina's culture. Don't knock it.

SITUATION 2

It's August and you've been invited for a few days' skiing in Bariloche, The weather forecast predicted lots of snow and freezing temperatures. You plan to fly there and want to take only one small suitcase as hand luggage. What do you pack?

A Woolly jumpers, a down jacket, long johns, gloves and anything else chunky and unattractive. Nothing really matches, but what does it matter, this is the middle of Patagonia and you're going to the mountains! Surely the fashion police won't be there?

❸ Skimp on warm clothes to leave plenty of space for slinky dresses/ dinner jackets, your best party shoes and some alka seltzer.

❸ One great ski suit and a fantastic evening outfit that will knock the socks off your hosts.

Comments

❹, of course, seems to be the obvious choice: August is the height of winter in Argentina and in this neck of the woods things can get quite chilly. But wait a minute! Are you not forgetting that you're in Argentina and must be fairly fashionable at all times—especially in a resort like Bariloche where you're bound to rub shoulders with the *farándula*? Going out is big business in Bariloche; people aren't here just for the skiing but for the string of discos and nights of revelling. You will definitely need something great to wear in the evenings. ❸ means you close off your skiing options. ❸ is the ideal solution (although maybe you should pack that alka seltzer after all).

SITUATION 3

You are attending a carnival party in an old barn off the beaten track somewhere in the northwest. You've just washed your hair and are wearing your best outfit when a member of the opposite sex, whom you've never met before, pinches your bottom and sprays fake snow in your hair. Do you:

❹ Dash off and buy a can of spray snow, seek out the perpetrator and gleefully avenge yourself?

❸ Book yourself into some psychoanalysis, fearing that you'll never understand male/female relationships?

❸ Leave the room in tears?

Comments

Take it as a compliment, but not as a literal come-on. Carnival is a flirtatious time, and Argentines are outrageous flirts. ❸ won't get you anywhere, you'll just miss out on a great party where behaviour like this is perfectly acceptable—it only happens once a year after all. Seeing a psychoanalyst, **B**, wouldn't be that inappropriate. You'll be surprised how many other Argentines do—though probably not for these reasons. **A**, of course is the best answer. It's amazing how therapeutic a can of fake snow and a few drinks can be.

SITUATION 4

In Argentina on business, you're running on a tight schedule and the current meeting is beginning to drag. Five minutes into the talks you were pretty sure this wasn't for you, you don't want to cut a deal and you have another business appointment lined up across town in 10 minutes. You're starting to feel frustrated and want to leave. Do you:

A Make a bolt for the door at the first possible moment, murmuring your apologies on your way out?

B Let the chief Argentine in the group bring the meeting to an end, remain for a few more minutes of small talk, and roll up 15 minutes late for your next appointment?

C Keep glancing at your watch and eventually—when they haven't got the message—lose your cool and stalk out in a huff?

Comments

A is not a good choice. By running off, you're implying that your next engagement is more important than the present company and it will be taken as an insult. **C** would be a big mistake. You're burning your bridges if you leave under a black cloud. The Argentine business world is a fairly close-knit community and word of your attitude is likely to get around, closing doors to you in future business negotiations. **B** may be the only possible solution. In the future you'll know not to schedule back-to-back meetings.

SITUATION 5

A friend invites you to the local *milonga* in San Telmo. The catch is, you've never danced the tango before. You are scared of making an idiot of yourself, so do you:

ⓐ Throw your inhibitions aside, rush out and get dressed in the full tango kit (fishnets/trilby, scarlet lipstick/wet look hair gel), then leap onto the dance floor as soon as you arrive?

ⓑ Accept, secretly knowing that absolutely no one is going to get you on that dance floor?

ⓒ Politely decline the offer and spend the evening kicking your heels at home, miserable?

Comments

None of the answers is a real winner. Only absolute wallflowers should choose option **ⓒ**. Tango isn't the exclusive preserve of professional ballroom dancers. Besides, a *milonga* is a great place to drink, people-watch and dance. **ⓐ** may be overly enthusiastic. It's certainly fun to dress up occasionally but you'll look a trifle silly if you arrive in full fancy dress and don't know where to put your feet. **ⓑ** is a possibility, but don't get put off giving the dance a shot—especially if you're female. An experienced tango dancer should be able to guide you across the floor with no trouble. For men it may be harder, but you've got to start somewhere after all.

If you really lack confidence a number of dance halls hold two-hour classes before the real dancing begins. Go early, learn the rudimentary steps and then dance the night away.

SITUATION 6

You've bravely stepped out to cross Avenida Nueve de Julio in Buenos Aires—the world's widest road. A little green man had given you the all-clear, but at the last minute a car shoots the red light and misses you by an inch. Do you:

ⓐ Scream from the top of your voice every Argentine obscenity you know, telling the driver exactly what you think of his mother?

ⓑ Raise both your hands in the air in an exasperated gesture—fingers bunched together, jabbing skyward?

ⓒ Meekly retreat to the safety of the pavement and wait for the lights to change again before cautiously attempting the crossing a second time?

Comments

Ⓐ will go unheard by the motorist and you'll probably just end up horrifying your fellow pedestrians with your bad language. **Ⓑ** is the best response, since he'll see your sign language in his rear-view mirror (if he bothers to look), and you'll have given vent to a bit of that frustration physically. **Ⓒ** is an understandable response for the pedestrian novice on Argentina's roads, but you're not going to get very far with that sort of attitude in Buenos Aires. Aggressive motorists have given rise to equally pushy pedestrians and unless you plan to confine yourself to just one half of Buenos Aires you are going to have to get used to crossing all 20 lanes of Nueve de Julio sooner or later.

DO'S AND DON'TS

DO'S

- Accept an invitation to drink *mate*. It's not just a drink; it's a social ritual.
- Drink the local red wines with your steak. A better gastronomic combination is hard to find.
- Try the *chinchulines*, *morcilla*, and other innards on the menu, even if it's just the once.
- Make an effort with your appearance. Argentines are incredibly image-conscious.
- Learn to gesticulate when you talk. You'll fit right in, and it's a wonderfully easy way to express yourself.
- Dance the tango in Buenos Aires.
- Make an effort to get out of Buenos Aires. The countryside is spectacular.
- Kiss friends on the cheek to greet them hello and goodbye.
- Take care on Argentina's roads, whether you are the driver or the pedestrian.
- Wear a seatbelt, even if no one else does. Argentina has a dreadful record for traffic fatalities.
- Keep your patience with bureaucrats. Foot stamping and threats will get you nowhere.
- Always make sure you have a plentiful supply of small change in your purse (100 peso notes are near impossible to change).
- Get swept up in Boca-River football madness.
- Use all contacts and networking opportunities to your full advantage. Everyone else does.
- Visit an *estancia* and see the gauchos at work. This is the real heart of Argentina.

DON'TS

- Worry if you can't speak Spanish. You'll learn fast with practice, and many Argentines also speak very good English.

- Go out for dinner before 9 pm. You'll probably be the only person in the restaurant. Argentines eat late.
- Go to a nightclub before 2 am. It's simply not cool.
- Arrive dead on time. You'll be early.
- Mention the Malvinas, military dictatorships, and other sensitive issues, at least not in a first meeting.
- Let the *mañana* syndrome—the art of putting things off till tomorrow—always get the upper-hand. Occasionally, it pays to stand your ground.
- Be overly aggressive in business. Your Argentine colleagues will offer (and expect) a bit of wining and dining.
- Get flustered about *piropos* (cat calls and wolf whistles) while walking down the street. But do ignore them.
- Get upset with any nicknames that may be hoisted upon you. Everyone falls victim sooner or later.
- Be offended by candid comments. Argentines believe in being open, frank, and direct.
- Get into a taxi without checking the driver's ID first (it hangs from the back of his seat in a plastic cover). Better still, call for a *remise* (minicab) from a reputable company.
- Get too upset about smoking. It's not the cultural taboo that it is back home.
- Get too sucked in by the thin culture/plastic surgery/ psychoanalysis fads prevalent in Buenos Aires.

GLOSSARY

Spanish	English
ACA	Automóvil Club Argentino (Argentine Automobile Club)
albergue transitorio	motel, usually where lovers meet
alfajor	a much loved type of biscuit
argentinidad	Argentinity; the essential Argentine national character
asado	a barbecue like no other you'll have seen before
asador	the man that does the barbecuing
bandoneón	an accordion like instrument used in the music of the tango
barra brava	organised group of football hooligans, often armed and looking for a fight
BsAs	acronym for Buenos Aires
bife	beef
bodega	winery
boleadoras	weighted balls on a leather strap used as a weapon by gauchos to bring down their prey
bombilla	metal (often silver) straw used to drink *mate*
cacerolazo	name given to the collective street demonstrations, accompanied by the deafening clanking of pots and pans, that first occurred in December 2001 eventually bringing down the presidency of Fernando de la Rua
Capital Federal	another term for the city of Buenos Aires

Spanish	English
castellano	literally 'castilian', the type of Spanish spoken in Latin America
cebador	term for the man or woman who serves *mate*
che	universal term of address
Clásico (el)	the classic football match between the great rival teams of Boca Juniors and River Plate
coima	bribe
coimero	one who solicits a bribe
colectivo	local/city bus
combi	long-distance bus
compañero	comrade, companion, colleague
confitería	café that also serves light meals
countries (los)	gated suburban communities
criollo	Argentine native
Dirty War	term used to describe the attack on Argentine civilians by the military dictatorships of the 1970s and 1980s in which an estimated 30,000 people disappeared
desaparecidos	the 'disappeared', the victims of Argentina's Dirty War whose bodies were never found
doma	rodeo
dulce de leche	sweet, sticky caramel spread used in countless biscuits and pastries
estancia	country ranch often of many thousands of hectares in size
facón	traditional gaucho knife
farándula	Argentina's celebrity jet set

Spanish	English
gauchada	a favour, a spontaneous act of generosity
gaucho	historically Argentina's cowboy, now used to describe a ranch hand
gauchesco	gaucho poetry depicting rural life in Argentina
gringo	a non-Latin American foreigner (usually a North American or European)
hora inglesa/hora americana	the use of English/American timing implying punctuality
Interior (el)	anywhere in Argentina outside Buenos Aires city
Islas Malvinas (las)	the Falkland Islands
IVA	*impuesto de valor agregado*, value-added tax
locutorio	telephone office where you can make local/long distance calls, send faxes and access the Internet
lunfardo	street slang of Buenos Aires
machismo	a very Latin form of male chauvinism
mate	traditional drink of green tea on which most Argentines are hooked, also refers to the gourd in which the tea is prepared (see also *yerba mate*)
marea roja	the 'red tide' a particularly lethal phenomenon which affects the local shellfish making them poisonous to human consumption

Spanish	English
mestizo	of mixed race, having Spanish and indigenous blood
milonga	a tango song or dance as well as the tango dance salon itself
pampero	fierce windstorm of the pampas
parrilla	grill restaurant, steak house
parrillada	grill, barbecue
pasaperros	professional dog walkers, a common sight in Buenos Aires
paseo	a walk/promenade or an outing
pato	a traditional gaucho game played at great speed on horseback in which opposing teams contest the possession of a duck (now a ball) in a leather bag
payador	singer of improvisational songs
peón	agricultural labourer, cowhand or ranch worker
peronista	a supporter of Juan Domingo Perón and the Peronist party
piso	floor
piropo	suggestive comment, catcall
porteño	a resident of Buenos Aires
Proceso (El)	the process by which the military juntas waged a bloody war against supposed subversives resulting in the death of an estimated 30,000 people (see also Dirty War)
propina	tip
pueblo	village or small town
pulpería	rural general store/tavern
quebrada	a canyon

Spanish	English
quinceañera	the fifteenth birthday—a big celebration for Argentine girls
quinta	country house in its own grounds
recargo	a surcharge, usually of about 10 percent, that many Argentine businesses add to credit card transactions
remise	a private taxi
s/n	short for '*sin numero*' indicating a street address without numbers
sobremesa	after lunch/after dinner conversation around the dining table
sortija	equestrian ring race
Subte (el)	Buenos Aires' underground train system
tanguero	a tango aficionado
tenedor libre	all you can eat
truco	popular card game
viaje de egresados	holiday taken by a group of students on their graduation
villa miseria	shantytown
viveza criolla	native cunning
voseo	in grammar, the use of the *vos* form instead of the *tu*' form in the second person singular
yerba mate	a type of green tea made from the plant Ilex paraguarensis, also known as Jesuit tea (see also *mate*)
zonda	a hot dry wind that blows off the Andes

RESOURCE GUIDE

Contacts are everything in Argentina. You can never know too many people (and their telephone numbers). Strings are pulled, friends of friends and cousins of cousins are called for help. Recommendations come best by word-of-mouth, but should you arrive cold and 'contactless', I hope the following will be of some help.

EMERGENCIES AND HEALTH
Emergency Numbers
- Police: 101
- Fire: 100
- Ambulance: 107
- Environmental emergency: 105
- Coast guard: 106

The Argentine police also operate a 24-hour police helpline in English for tourists requiring police assistance on 0800-999-5000

Hospitals
The following private hospitals have English-speaking staff. In each neighbourhood, pharmacies take it in turn to remain open during the night, so you can get hold of medicines and prescriptions round-the-clock. Look in the local newspapers under Farmacias del Turno.
- Hospital Aleman (German Hospital)
  Pueyreddon 1640, (1118) Capital Federal
  Tel: (011) 4821-1700.
- Hospital Britanico (British Hospital)
  Perdriel 74, (1280) Capital Federal
  Tel: (011) 4309-6500.
- Hospital Italiano (Italian Hospital)
  Gascón 450, Capital Federal
  Tel: (011) 4959-0200.

Dental Clinics

There are both private and public dental services. Prices vary, but a filling will probably cost about US$ 50. In Buenos Aires, try:

- Hospital de Odontologia
  Pueyreddon 940, Capital Federal
  Tel: (011) 4805-6407
  This public dental hospital is open 24 hours a day, and no appointment is necessary.

TRANSPORT AND COMMUNICATIONS
Mail

When writing addresses, the number follows the street name, and the postal code generally precedes the city name, which precedes the province name. Here are some common terms and abbreviations:

Avenida, or Av, or Avda	Avenue
Calle	Street
Esquina, or Esq	Corner
Edificio, or Edif	Building
Oficina, or Of	Office
Piso, or P (Planta Baja, or PB)	Floor (Ground floor)
Bs.As or BA	Buenos Aires, province
Capital Federal, or CF	Buenos Aires, city
Casilla (de Correo), or CC	Post office box
Codigal Postal, or CP	Postal code
Sin Numero or s/n	No number
Telf	Telephone

Telephone

The international country code for calling Argentina is + + 54. Dial 19 for the national operator; for an international operator dial 000. The city dialing codes are:

- Buenos Aires: 011
- Bahia Blanca: 0291
- Catamarca: 03833
- Córdoba: 0351

- Corrientes: 0373
- La Rioja: 03822
- Mendoza: 0261
- Paraná: 0343
- Rawson: 02965
- Rio Gallegos: 02966
- Salta: 0387
- San Luis: 02652
- Santa Fé: 0342
- Santiago del Estero: 0385
- Ushuaia: 02901

- Formosa: 03717
- Mar de Plata: 0223
- Neuquén: 0299
- Posadas: 03752
- Resistencia: 03722
- Rosario: 0341
- San Juan: 0264
- San Salvador de Jujuy: 03882
- Santa Rosa: 02954
- San Miguel de Tucumán: 0381
- Viedma: 02920

For national telephone directory inquiries, dial 110 (or check the local Yellow Pages at www.paginasamarillas.com.ar).

Internet

Computers and software are widely available in Argentina. Most *locutorios* (telephone centers) offer affordable Internet and fax services and there are numerous Internet cafes throughout the country. There is no shortage of Argentine-based Internet Service Providers (ISPs). The two most popular are Telefonica (http://www.telefonica.com.ar) and Arnet (http://www.arnet.com.ar).

EMBASSIES

- Australia
  Villanueva 1400, Buenos Aires CF.
  Tel: (011) 4779-3500
- Canada
  Tagle 2828, Buenos Aires CF.
  Tel: (011) 4808-1000
- France
  Santa Fe 846, 4th floor, Buenos Aires CF.
  Tel: (011) 4312-2409
- Germany
  Villanueva 1055, Buenos Aires.
  Tel: (011) 4778-2500
- Israel
  Av de Mayo 701, 10th floor, Buenos Aires CF
  Tel: (011) 4338-2500

- Italy
  Marcelo T Alvear 1125, Buenos Aires CF.
  Tel: (011) 4816-6132
- Japan
  Bouchard 547, 17th floor, Buenos Aires, CF
  Tel: (011) 4318-8200
- The Netherlands
  Olga Cossenttini 831, 3rd floor, Buenos Aires, CF
  Tel: (011) 4338-0050
- Spain
  Guido 1760, Buenos Aires, CF.
  Tel: (011) 4811-0070
- UK
  Dr Luis Agote 2412, Buenos Aires, CF.
  Tel: (011) 4808-2000
- USA
  Colombia 4300, Buenos Aires, CF.
  Tel: (011) 5777-4533

TRAVEL

If you're going to spend time in Buenos Aires, get hold of
the Guia T (bus guidebook), available at most newsstands
in the city for about US$1. It shows you all the bus routes in
Buenos Aires, with concise maps of the city. These stations
can provide train and bus details:

- Estación Retiro (Retiro train station)
  Av Ramos Mejía, Capital Federal
  Tel: (011) 4317-4407
  Suburban services and some long-distance (but erratic)
  services to Rosario, Santa Fe, and Tucumán.
- Estación Once (Once train station)
  Tel: (0800) 333-3822
  Suburban services and rail links to Santa Rosa.
- Estación Constitución (Constitución train station)
  General Hornos 11, Capital Federal
  Tel: (011) 4304-0028
  Services between BA and Mar del Plata and other
  destinations in BA.

- Estación Terminal Retiro (Long-distance bus station)
  Antártida Argentina and Ramos Mejía, Capital Federal
  Tel: (011) 4310-0700
  Bus/coach services to cities throughout Argentina.
- Manuel Tienda Leon (http://www.tiendaleon.com)
  Santa Fe 790, Capital Federal
  Tel: (011) 4315-5115
  Run buses connecting Ezeiza Airport with downtown
  Buenos Aires.

Airports and Airlines

Most of the major cities have airports. Most international
flights leave from Ezeiza [Tel: (011) 5480-6111], about 35km
south of BA. Most domestic flights and flights to Uruguay
leave from Aeroparque Jorge Newbery [Tel (011) 4514-1515], a
few kilometers north of downtown BA. These airlines provide
domestic flights:

- Aerolíneas Argentinas
  Perú 2, Capital Federal. Tel: (011) 4340-7777
  Website: http://www.aerolineas.com
- LADE
  Peru\' 710, Capital Federal
  Tel: (011) 5129-9000 or (0810) 810-5233
  Website: http://www.lade.com.ar

Boat

In Buenos Aires, Buquebus run regular ferries to Colonia and
Montevideo both in Uruguay.

- Buquebus
  Av Antártida Argentina 821. Tel: (011) 4316-6400
  Website: http://www.buquebus.com

Maps

Contact the Automovil Club Argentino for good road maps
for travel around the country and for mechanical assistance,
insurance, tour promotions, a driving school, and other
member benefits. Newspaper kiosks sell good national,
city, and provincial maps one of the best publications is
AUTOMAPA (http://www.automapa.com.ar). The Instituto

Geográfico Militar (Geographical Military Institute) is good for topographical maps and satellite images.

- Automovil Club Argentino
  Av Libertador 1850, (1425) Capital Federal
  Tel: (011) 4808-4640 / (0800) 888-9888
  Website: http://www.aca.org.ar
- The Instituto Geográfico Militar
  Av Cabildo 381, Capital Federal
  Tel: (011) 4576-5576
  Website: http://www.geoargentina.com.ar

ACCOMMODATION

Local tourist offices will be able to provide you with listings of hotels. The following websites are all good options if you want long/short term rents or even are looking to buy your own property. They also specialize on luxury rentals: htttp://www.apartmentsba.com; htttp://www.andinoproperty.com and htttp://www. argentinahomes.com

LANGUAGE SCHOOLS

The University of Buenos Aires holds Spanish courses for foreigners. Apply to the Centro Universitario de Idiomas. A number of private instructors advertise daily in the *Buenos Aires Herald* classifieds. You'll find a comprehensive listing of Spanish study programmes in Argentina at http://www.spanishcourses.info and www.spanarg.org.

- Centro Universitario de Idiomas
  Av Cordoba 2636, Capital Federal.
  Tel: (011) 4816-0964)

ENTERTAINMENT AND LEISURE
Libraries

The Biblioteca Lincoln has the New York Times, Washington Post, and books and magazines in English.

- The Biblioteca Lincoln
  Maipú 672, Capital Federal
  Tel: (011) 5382-1536)
  Website: http://www.bcl.edu.ar

Museums

Some 500 museums are listed, with opening hours and price information, at http://www.museosargentinos.org.ar

Restaurants and Cafés

Most restaurants and cafés in Argentina are good, but it's best to get a word-of-mouth recommendation. If in doubt, opt for a *parrilla* (steak house) and order the beef (you can't go wrong on this one). To soak up some classic *porteño* atmosphere while in BA, two cafés I can't resist are the Confitería Ideal (Suipacha 384) and Café Tortoni (Av de Mayo 825). Both have stacks of atmosphere and great coffee.

Shopping

Argentina is good for shopping, especially for quality leather goods and silverware. Buenos Aires can easily compete with European rivals for shops. All the major cities have sparkling shopping malls. A good place to start is Calle Florida in BA. Argentina uses European shoe and clothing sizes. At the airport, you can recover the 21 per cent value-added tax if you spend more than $ 200 (per invoice) on local products in shops that are members of this scheme.

Sports and Cultural Associations

Get up-to-date tournament news and background information on polo clubs and players in Argentina from the Asociación Argentina de Polo.

The National Tango Academy has leaflets with information on Buenos Aires' happening tango scene

- Asociación Argentina de Polo
  Are\'valo 3065, Capital Federal.
  Tel: (011) 4777-6444
  Website: http://www.aapolo.com
- The National Tango Academy
  Palacio Carlos Gardel, Avda de Mayo 833,
  (1084) Capital Federal. Tel: (011) 4345-6968
  Website: http://www.anacdeltango.org.ar
- Argentine Golf Association
  Av Corrientes 538, Piso 11, (1043) Capital Federal

Tel: (011) 4325-1113
Website: http://www.aag.com.ar

Alternative Lifestyles

For gay and lesbian information, look out for free magazines including *Queer X*, *Latino* and *La Otra Guia* available at most gay bars, cafes and discos. For up-to-date info on Buenos Aires' annual gay pride parade go to http://www.marchdelorgullo. org.ar. One of Argentina's best gay websites (in English) can be found at http://www.thegayguide.com.ar

Newspapers, Magazines, Books and Media

Thanks to Argentina's considerable Anglophile community, English reading material is readily available, although it may come at a price. If you poke around into the further recesses of Argentina's famous bookshops you'll also come across books in French, Portuguese, German and Italian. There is an English-language daily newspaper, the *Buenos Aires Herald* (www.buenosaireshrald.com), with good coverage of national and international news, finance and sports. You'll also be able to pick up any number of English and American magazines from *Vogue* to the *Economist* at newspaper kiosks in the larger cities. For Spanish readers, newspaper kiosks are packed with every possible type of magazine from Tango to Travel. Businessmen will want to devour the pages of the business dailies *Ambito Financiero* or *El Cronista*. *El Clarin* and *La Nacion* all of which are also online. Cable television is popular in Argentina, but national TV stations are also good with amusing chat shows, riveting *telenovelas* (soap operas), current affairs documentaries and news. If a football match is being televised, however, think twice before trying to change channels—especially if there's a man in the room.

BUSINESS INFORMATION
Business Organisations

The *Fundacion Invertir* has a useful website for those doing business with or in Argentina at www.invertir.com. Other useful contacts include:

- Argentine Chamber of Commerce
  Av L.N. Alem 36, (1003) Capital Federal
  Tel: (011) 5300-9000. Fax: (011) 5300-9058
  Website: http://www.cac.com.ar
- Buenos Aires Stock Exchange
  Saramiento 299, Piso 1, (1353) Capital Federal
  Tel: (011) 4316-7000
  Website: http://www.bcba.sba.com.ar
- Ministry of Foreign Affairs, International Trade,
  and Worship
  Esmeralda 1212, Capital Federal. Tel: (011) 4819-7000
  Website: http://www.mrecic.gov.ar
- *Fundación Exportar*
  Reconquista 1098, (1003) Capital Federal
  Tel: (011) 4315-4125
  Website: http://www.fundacionexportar.org.ar
  Trade information and opportunities.

Legal Services

Contact the Argentine Bar Federation (FCAC) for details of law firms in Argentina.

- Argentine Bar Federation (FCAC)
  Av de Mayo 651 in Buenos Aires. Tel: (011) 4331-8009

Managing Your Money
Taxes

Argentine companies register their employees with the tax authority and retain taxes from employee salaries. If you are self-employed, contact the *Dirección General Impositiva*.

- *Dirección General Impositiva* (Argentine Tax Bureau)
  Avenida Paseo Colón 635, Capital Federal
  Tel: (011) 4331-7807

Insurance

- *Asociación Argentina de Compañías de Seguros* (Argentine Association of Insurance Companies)
  25 de Mayo 565, (1002) Capital Federal
  Tel: (011) 4313-6974. Fax: (011) 4312-6300).

Cash and Credit

You won't have trouble changing currencies at banks and *casas de cambio*, though they will charge a small fee. Cashing traveler's cheques is something else altogether. No one's interested in them, and if you do find a willing bank, expect high commissions. ATMs are handier and common in the cities. They can also be used for cash advances on major credit cards such as MasterCard and Visa. American Express Diners Card is also valid in many places. Many businesses add a 10 % surcharge on credit card purchases.

RELIGION AND VOLUNTEER WORK
Volunteer Organisations

Visit www.volunteerabroad.com and click on Argentina for a list of volunteer opportunities in Argentina.

Religious Organisations

The *Agencia Informativa Cátolica Argentina* provides links and information on the Catholic Church in Argentina. The Muslim community can visit www.organizacionislam.org. ar for news and information. The Jewish community can visit www.shalomonline.com for news, views, and general information or contact the AMIA for social and educational assistance.

- *Agencia Informativa Cátolica Argentina*
  Bolívar 218, (1066) Capital Federal
  Tel: (011) 4343-4397
  Website: http://www.aica.org
- AMIA
  Pasteur 633, (1024) Capital Federal
  Tel: (011) 4959-8800
  Website: http://www.amia.org.ar

TOURIST OFFICES AND IMMIGRATION
Tourist Offices

Government tourist offices around the country can supply regional information and a list of *casas de familia* and local *estancias*. Contact the *Secretaria de Turismo de la Nación*.

- *Secretaria de Turismo de la Nación*
  Santa Fe 883, (1059) Capital Federal
  Tel: 0800 50016
  Website: http://www.turismo.gov.ar

Immigration and Residency

If you plan to stay longer than 90 days in Argentina, you should contact the *Dirección Nacional de Migraciones*. They can also organise work and residence visas within Argentina although it is always advisable to apply for visas in your home country before coming to Argentina.

- *Dirección Nacional de Migraciones*
  Av Antártida Argentina 1335, Capital Federal
  Tel: (011) 4317-0234 / 0800 333 728-742
  Website: http://www.migraciones.gov.ar

FURTHER READING

HISTORY

One of the best and most concise history books on Argentina is Argentina 1516 to 1987 (David Rock, University of California Press, 1985). Alternatively try A House Divided: Argentina 1880–1980 (Eduardo Crawley, C. Hurst and Co, 1984).

You will find no shortage of books on Juan Domingo Perón and his wife Evita. Try *Perón: A Biography* (Joseph Page, Random House, 1983) and *Evita: An Intimate Portrait of Eva Perón* (Tomás De Elia et al, Rizzoli, 1997) or the more critical *Evita: Saint or Sinner* (W.A. Harbinson, Forge, 1996). Both the semi-fictionalised *Santa Evita* (Tomás Eloy Martínez, Vintage, 1997) and *The Perón Novel* (Tomás Eloy Martínez, Vintage, 1999) make for enjoyable reading. *Santa Evita*, especially, is a must for those who want a better understanding of Argentina's obsession with the dead. Also see the non-fictional essay *The Return of Eva Perón* (V.S. Naipaul, Andre Deutsch, 1980).

The Dirty War and military dictatorships are explored in greater detail in *Argentina's Lost Patrol: Armed Struggle* 1969–1979 (Maria Jose Moyano, Yale University Press, 1995). The book is based on interviews with military and political leaders, guerrillas and journalists. Also see *A State of Fear: Memories of Argentina's Nightmare* (Andrew Graham Yooll, London, Eland Books, 1986) written by the editor-in-chief of the Buenos Aires Herald, who was forced into exile in 1976. He is also the author of *Committed Observer: Memoirs of a Journalist* (Andrew Graham Yooll, John Libby and Co, 1995).

Nunca Mas (Faber and Faber, 1986) is the official report by Argentina's National Commission on Disappeared People. One of the founding mothers of the Plaza de Mayo provides a moving account of the mothers' testimonies in *Circle of Love over Death* (Matilde Mellibovsky, Connecticut, Curbstone Press, 1997). *I Remember Julia: Voices of the Disappeared* (Eric Steiner Carlson, Temple University Press, 1996) traces the life of a disappeared doctor and mother-to-be through eyewitness accounts. The novel Imagining *Argentina* (Lawrence Thornton, Bantam, 1991) is set during the Dirty War and explores the life of a man whose wife has disappeared.

The Battle for the Falklands (Max Hastings and Simon Jenkins, W.W. Norton and Co, 1984) gives a concise account of the 1982 South Atlantic War, or try the shorter *Argentine Forces in the Falklands* (Nicholas Van Der Bijl, Osprey, 1993). A British journalist, who was in Argentina during and after the Falklands War, provides an interesting account of the post-war years in The Land that lost its Heroes: *The Falklands, The Post War and Alfonsín* (Jimmy Burns, Bloomsbury, 1987).

A lesser known side of Argentina's history is explored in *The Afro-Argentines of Buenos Aires, 1800–1900* (George Reid Andrews, University of Wisconsin Press, 1980). The history of the Welsh is recorded in great detail in *The Desert and the Dream: A Study of Welsh Colonisation in Chubut* (Glyn Williams, University of Wales Press, 1975). The same author also wrote *The Welsh in Patagonia* (Glyn Williams, University of Wales Press, 1991).

GAUCHOS

For everything and anything you ever wanted to know about Argentina's gauchos, don't miss *Gauchos and the Vanishing Frontier* (Richard W. Slatta, University of Nebraska Press, 1992). The epic poem *El Gaucho Martín Fierro*, written by José Hernández in the 1870s, is now considered a masterpiece and is by far the most widely read and discussed work produced in Argentina. It traces the problems faced by the gaucho, forced to yield his freedom and individuality to the social and material changes invading the pampas in the late 1800s. Translated editions are also available including *The Gaucho Martin Fierro* (José Hernández, translated by Frank G Carrino, Alberto J Carlos and Norman Mangouni, Scholars Facsimilies & Reprint, 1999). *Don Segundo Sombra* (Ricardo Güiraldes, Mestas Ediciones, 2006) is another great gaucho classic. First published in 1926, it also laments the loss of the romantic gaucho.

TRAVEL

In Patagonia (Bruce Chatwin, Penguin, 1988) is an unbeatable travel book on Patagonia and has been dubbed the book that redefined travel writing. Also see *An Englishman in Patagonia* (John Pilkington, Century, 1991) with assorted adventures including taking tea with the Welsh and discovering more about the North American bandits Butch Cassidy and the Sundance Kid, who briefly set up home in Patagonia. Their lives and South American skirmishes are explored in impeccable detail in *Digging Up Butch and Sundance* (Anne Meadows, University of Nebraska Press, 1996).

Another excellent travel book is the funny but melancholic *Bad Times in Buenos Aires* (Miranda France, London, Weidenfeld and Nicolson, 1998). *The Drunken Forest* (Gerald Durrell, `house of Stratus, 2001) and *The Whispering Land* (Gerald Durrell, Penguin, 2006) are also great travelogues.

Backpackers and the more adventurous travellers out there should get their hands on *Backpacking and Hiking in Chile* and *Argentina* (Tim Burford and Andrew Dixon, Bradt, 2001) and *Trekking in the Patagonian Andes* (Clem Lindenmayer and Nick Tapp, Lonely Planet Publications, 2003). And both the *Lonely Planet and Footprint Handbook* guides on Argentina provide good and comprehensive lists of hotels, tours and travel in Argentina. Also see the *Insight Guide on Argentina*, which has good cultural sections and fantastic colour photographs.

The Voyage of the Beagle (Charles Darwin, Wordsworth Editions Ltd, 1997) may be quite outdated but still makes for great reading, following the naturalist in his South American travels. *Uttermost Part of the Earth* (E. Lucas Bridges, Hodder and Stoughton, 1948; Dutton, 1949) is an arresting account by the missionary Thomas Bridges' son on life growing up in Tierra del Fuego with Yamana Indians. *Far Away and Long Ago* (W.H. Hudson, Eland, 2005) is a book of nostalgic reminiscences of a childhood in the pampas, an absolute must for bird fans. Born in Argentina in 1841, Hudson also wrote *Idle days in Patagonia* (W.H. Hudson, Nonsuch Publishing, 2005) and *A Naturalist in La Plata* (W.H. Hudson, Dover, 1994).

NATURAL HISTORY

Birdwatchers should get their hands on *A Guide to the Birds of South America* (Rodolphe Meyer de Schauensee, Atlantic Books, 1982) or *Birds of Southern South America and Antarctica* (by Martin R.de la Pena and Maurice Rumboli, HarperCollins, 1998). *A Guide to the Birds and Mammals of Coastal Patagonia* (Graham Harris and William Conway, Princeton University Press, 1998) is also a good directory of the region's fauna.

Packed with colour photographs, *Argentine Trout Fishing: A Fly Fisherman's Guide to Patagonia* (William C. Leitch, Frank Amato, 1991) is more than just an angling guide, taking the reader on a comprehensive tour of Patagonia's rivers, streams and lakes, and giving useful practical tips.

LITERATURE

No bibliography on Argentina would be complete without mentioning that country's greatest writers. The works of Jorge Luis Borges (1899–1986) reflect the changing character of Argentine development and include *Labyrinths* (Jorge Luis Borges, Penguin, 2000) *Brodies' Report* (Jorge Luis Borges, Penguin, 2005), *A Universal History of Iniquity* (Jorge Luis Borges, Penguin, 2006), *The Book of Sand* (Jorge Luis Borges, Penguin, 2001) and *The Aleph* (Jorge Luis Borges, Penguin, 2000). Other 20th century Argentine writers to look out for are Adolfo Bioy Casares, Tomás Eloy Martínez, Ernesto Sabato (*On Heroes and Tombs and El Tunel*) and Manuel Puig (*Kiss of the Spider Woman*, *Betrayed by Rita Hayworth*, *Heartbreak Tango*, *The Buenos Aires Affair* and *Eternal Curse on the Reader of These Pages*).

Also don't miss out on the works of one of Argentina's most famous writers, Julio Cortázar, whose works include *Los Premios*, *Rayuela* (Hopscotch), *62*, *La Vuelta al Dia en Ochenta Mundos* and *Queremos tanto a Glenda*.

BUSINESS

Business visitors will find Argentina Business: *The portable Encyclopedia for Doing Business with Argentina* (California, The World Trade Press, 1996, 1998) indispensable. Price Waterhouse also published a booklet, *Doing Business in*

Argentina (Price Waterhouse World Film Services BV, Inc, 1995). Also see *Argentina Investment & Business Guide* by *Emerging Markets Investment Center* (International Business Publications USA, updated annually).

BIOGRAPHIES

The rise and fall of Argentina's football star, Diego Maradona, is explored in detail in *Hand of God, The Life of Diego Maradona* (Jimmy Burns, Bloomsbury, 2002). This is the unauthorised version and apparently Maradona wasn't too pleased about it.

For the definitive biography on Argentina's prodigal son, read *Che Guevara—A Revolutionary Life* (Jon Lee Anderson, London, Transworld Publishers Ltd, 1997). The early chapters also give an extraordinary insight into Argentina during the early 20th century. Guevara's own account of his motorcycle trip across South America, including Argentina, is revealed in *The Motorcycle Diaries* (Ernesto Che Guevara, HarperPerennial 2004). *The Life, Music and Times of Carlos Gardel* (Simon Collier, University of Pittsberg Press, 1986) is a good biography of Argentina's greatest tango singer. And for a biography on the great man himself, see *Borges: A Life* (James Woodall, Basic Books, 1998) and *With Borges* (Alberto Manguel, Telegram Books, 2006).

FOOD AND WINE

Ending on a more bacchanalian note, *Wine Routes of Argentina* (Alan Young, International Wine Academy, 1998) is a good introduction to Argentina's wine industry. *Food and Drink in Argentina* (Dereck Foster and Richard Tripp, Aromas y Sabores Publishing, 2006) is another useful guide.

ABOUT THE AUTHOR

Fiona Adams was born in London in 1973 and has a degree in Archaeology and Anthropology and a Master's in Latin American Studies.

She worked as a journalist in Bolivia and Argentina and now lives in the Scottish Highlands with her husband Jamie and young son Tom.

250

INDEX

Titles in the CULTURE**SHOCK**! series:

Argentina	Hawaii	Paris
Australia	Hong Kong	Philippines
Austria	Hungary	Portugal
Bahrain	India	Russia
Barcelona	Indonesia	San Francisco
Beijing	Iran	Saudi Arabia
Belgium	Ireland	Scotland
Bolivia	Israel	Sri Lanka
Borneo	Italy	Shanghai
Brazil	Jakarta	Singapore
Britain	Japan	South Africa
Cambodia	Korea	Spain
Canada	Laos	Sweden
Chicago	London	Switzerland
Chile	Malaysia	Syria
China	Mauritius	Taiwan
Costa Rica	Mexico	Thailand
Cuba	Morocco	Tokyo
Czech Republic	Munich	Turkey
Denmark	Myanmar	Ukraine
Ecuador	Nepal	United Arab
Egypt	Netherlands	Emirates
Finland	New York	USA
France	New Zealand	Vancouver
Germany	Norway	Venezuela
Greece	Pakistan	Vietnam

For more information about any of these titles, please contact any of our Marshall Cavendish offices around the world (listed on page ii) or visit our website at:

www.marshallcavendish.com/genref